Fundamentals of Investment Appraisal

An Illustration based on a Case Study

Prof. Dr. Martina Röhrich
School of International Business of Bremen
University of Applied Sciences

R. Oldenbourg Verlag München Wien

Bibliografische Information der Deutschen Nationalbibliothek

Die Deutsche Nationalbibliothek verzeichnet diese Publikation in der Deutschen Nationalbibliografie; detaillierte bibliografische Daten sind im Internet über <http://dnb.d-nb.de> abrufbar.

© 2007 Oldenbourg Wissenschaftsverlag GmbH
Rosenheimer Straße 145, D-81671 München
Telefon: (089) 45051-0
oldenbourg.de

Das Werk einschließlich aller Abbildungen ist urheberrechtlich geschützt. Jede Verwertung außerhalb der Grenzen des Urheberrechtsgesetzes ist ohne Zustimmung des Verlages unzulässig und strafbar. Das gilt insbesondere für Vervielfältigungen, Übersetzungen, Mikroverfilmungen und die Einspeicherung und Bearbeitung in elektronischen Systemen.

Lektorat: Wirtschafts- und Sozialwissenschaften, wiso@oldenbourg.de
Herstellung: Anna Grosser
Satz: DTP-Vorlagen der Autorin
Coverentwurf: Kochan & Partner, München
Coverausführung: Gerbert-Satz, Grasbrunn
Gedruckt auf säure- und chlorfreiem Papier
Gesamtherstellung: Druckhaus „Thomas Müntzer" GmbH, Bad Langensalza

ISBN 978-3-486-58225-3

Contents

Preface		ix
Abbreviations and Symbols		xi
1	**An Introduction to the Investment Decision**	**1**
1.1	Learning Objectives	1
1.2	Case: Car Sharing Company	1
1.3	Investment Decisions and Business Finance	2
1.4	Classification of Investments and Stages of the Investment Process	3
1.5	Investment Appraisal Techniques	3
1.6	Summary and Evaluation	5
1.7	Exercises with Answers	5
1.7.1	Exercises	5
1.7.2	Answers	7
2	**Non-discounting Methods of Investment Appraisal**	**11**
2.1	Learning Objectives	11
2.2	Cost Comparison Method	11
2.2.1	Introduction	11
2.2.2	Comparison of Alternatives	12
2.2.3	Salvage Values	16
2.2.4	Critical Values	18
2.2.5	Replacement Decision	20
2.2.6	Evaluation of the Cost Comparison Method	24
2.3	Profit Comparison Method	24
2.3.1	Introduction	24
2.3.2	Comparison of Alternatives	25
2.3.3	Salvage Values	26
2.3.4	Critical Values	26
2.3.5	Replacement Decision	26
2.3.6	Evaluation of the Profit Comparison Method	28

2.4	Accounting Rate of Return Method	29
2.4.1	Introduction	29
2.4.2	Comparison of Alternatives	29
2.4.3	Salvage Values	30
2.4.4	Replacement Decision	31
2.4.5	Evaluation of the Accounting Rate of Return Method	32
2.5	Payback Method	33
2.5.1	Introduction	33
2.5.2	Comparison of Alternatives	33
2.5.3	Salvage Values	35
2.5.4	Replacement Decision	36
2.5.5	Evaluation of the Payback Method	37
2.6	Summary and Evaluation of the Non-Discounting Methods	37
2.7	Exercises with Answers	39
2.7.1	Exercises	39
2.7.2	Answers	45
3	**Discounting Methods of Investment Appraisal**	**55**
3.1	Learning Objectives	55
3.2	Time Value of Money	55
3.2.1	Basic Example	55
3.2.2	Compounding and Discounting	57
3.2.3	Future Value and Present Value of an Annuity	59
3.2.4	Annual Equivalent Factor and Sinking Fund Factor	60
3.2.5	Summary of Time Value of Money Calculations	61
3.3	Net Present Value Method	62
3.3.1	Introduction	62
3.3.2	Role of Financing	65
3.3.3	Relevance of Differential Investments	69
3.3.4	Comparison of Alternatives	72
3.3.5	Replacement Decision	73
3.3.6	Evaluation of the Net Present Value Method	75
3.4	Annuity Method	76
3.4.1	Introduction	76
3.4.2	Comparison of Alternatives	77
3.4.3	Replacement Decision	78
3.4.4	Evaluation of the Annuity Method	78
3.5	Internal Rate of Return Method	79
3.5.1	Introduction	79
3.5.2	Comparison of Alternatives	82
3.5.3	Internal Rate of Return versus Net Present Value	84
3.5.4	Evaluation of the Internal Rate of Return Method	87

3.6	Discounting Payback Method	87
3.6.1	Introduction	87
3.6.2	Comparison of Alternatives	87
3.6.3	Replacement Decision	89
3.6.4	Evaluation of the Discounting Payback Method	89
3.7	Summary and Evaluation of the Discounting Methods	89
3.8	Exercises with Answers	90
3.8.1	Exercises	90
3.8.2	Answers	95
4	**Investment Decision Making under Conditions of Uncertainty**	**109**
4.1	Learning Objectives	109
4.2	Uncertainty and Risk	110
4.3	Correction Method	111
4.3.1	Introduction	111
4.3.2	Comparison of Alternatives	112
4.3.3	Evaluation of the Correction Method	113
4.4	Sensitivity Analysis	114
4.4.1	Introduction	114
4.4.2	Comparison of Alternatives	114
4.4.3	Evaluation of the Sensitivity Analysis	117
4.5	Risk Analysis	118
4.5.1	Introduction	118
4.5.2	Comparison of Alternatives	119
4.5.3	Evaluation of the Risk Analysis	123
4.6	Decision Tree Analysis	123
4.6.1	Introduction	123
4.6.2	Comparison of Alternatives: Fixed Planning	124
4.6.3	Comparison of Alternatives: Flexible Planning	129
4.6.4	Evaluation of the Decision Tree Analysis	134
4.7	Summary and Evaluation	135
4.8	Exercises with Answers	135
4.8.1	Exercises	135
4.8.2	Answers	140
5	**Advanced Topics of Investment Appraisal**	**149**
5.1	Learning Objectives	149
5.2	Taxation	150
5.2.1	Introduction	150
5.2.2	Comparison of Alternatives	152
5.2.3	Evaluation of Taxation	154

5.3	Inflation	154
5.3.1	Introduction	154
5.3.2	Comparison of Alternatives	155
5.3.3	Evaluation of Inflation	157
5.4	Complete Financial Plan	157
5.4.1	Introduction	157
5.4.2	Comparison of Alternatives	158
5.4.3	Evaluation of the Complete Financial Plan	159
5.5	Scoring Model	160
5.5.1	Introduction	160
5.5.2	Comparison of Alternatives	161
5.5.3	Evaluation of the Scoring Model	163
5.6	Macroeconomic Net Present Value Method	163
5.6.1	Introduction	163
5.6.2	Comparison of Alternatives	165
5.6.3	Evaluation of the Macroeconomic Net Present Value Method	166
5.7	Summary and Evaluation	166
5.8	Exercises with Answers	167
5.8.1	Exercises	167
5.8.2	Answers	170
6	**Index of Questions and Solutions**	**175**
7	**References**	**179**
8	**Mathematical Tables**	**181**
9	**Index**	**189**

Preface

Investment appraisal is a subject which all students of economics or business are confronted with. This fact is sufficient for all students to make themselves familiar with its contents in order to pass the respective exams. According to their inclination toward and their interest in the topics of investment appraisal, students can either finish after the introductory courses or go on to advanced studies. The complexity of the material does not facilitate the students' comprehension of the topics. Possibly even the teachers spoil the students' interest in the subject by constantly changing methods and their mathematical derivations and abandon them after a while to a frustrating course of pure learning of facts.

In this context the idea for this book was conceived. It is based on long-term experience with students, especially at the School of International Business of Bremen University of Applied Sciences. While teaching classes and examining students I have often observed how difficult it is for them to get a straightforward feeling for the various methods of capital expenditure budgeting, having to evaluate the advantages and disadvantages of methods based on widely differing assumptions. Simple calculations made without a knowledge of the implicit assumptions of a given method, indeed, do not lead to the ability to choose the right method for solving a problem in investment appraisal. In this case a student can neither confidently face an oral exam nor can he or she later be able to decide on practical investments in real life. However, professional investment decisions are the basis for future success in a business environment. This, in fact, is the special significance of capital budgeting decisions.

Considering all the books about investment appraisal techniques already in existence, why do I want to add still another one? This book is consciously written in an easily understood style that gives the reader the opportunity to focus on the contents. I don't take for granted that you are already familiar with the subject matter. The reader, trying to grasp and understand this initially difficult subject, will be not be told that, after following "a few easy steps", the solutions are obvious. This book supplies you with a careful detailed explanation of the mathematical basics and does not assume previous knowledge of them. For a better understanding, a case study is constructed to illustrate all methods discussed. This case study focuses on the reality of student life as well as of practitioners: the founding of a car sharing enterprise.

In this book, a group of students carry out the founding, but this could also be the problem of a practitioner who wants to develop new areas of business. The goal of the book is to pace a sure way through the variety of methods. It is shown why there are different methods in investment appraisal and where to focus on in the given application. As all methods are introduced by the same case study, it is easy to compare and evaluate the results. The statements in the text are further consolidated by abstracts and evaluations of the respective methods as well as by exercises with extensive solutions.

Due to the increasing mobility of students and the internationalisation of many economic or business curricula, not only do German students tend to study more abroad, but also foreign students tend to study more in Germany. This trend leads to another group of readers which this book is directed at. In German universities the number of courses in the English language is also increasing. That is why I have written this text in English. A companion volume in German, entitled 'Grundlagen der Investitionsrechnung: Eine Darstellung anhand einer Fallstudie' is also available. In both textbooks the pages are constructed identically. Using both textbooks simultaneously will help those students who still lack the necessary business vocabulary in the respective language to reasonably follow a class in English or German.

In addition this book may help international students in attending courses in German. Thus it clearly closes an existing gap in the literature. To my knowledge, there is no book in English about capital expenditure budgeting in the sense as it is usually taught in German higher education institutions. As a result international students have no literature covering the contents of a course in investment appraisal. With the help of an easily readable case study with easily understood graphics and notations, students will be more interested and encouraged to study in Germany in the future.

Finally, I would like to thank the students of Bremen University of Applied Sciences who furnished the idea for this book by raising numerous critical questions. Their remarks and their discussions on the subject were the main reasons for the conception of this book as a case study. In addition, thanks to Dr. Rolf Jäger of Oldenbourg Verlag, Benjamin Hesse of the Hochschule Bremen and Anna Kessler who patiently accompanied the development of the manuscript. Last but not least my husband and my family deserve my special thanks for their patience.

Your comments and suggestions would be most welcome: mrochrich@hs-bremen.de

Martina Röhrich

Abbreviations and Symbols

A	Annuity
AEF	Annual equivalent factor
AK	Archimedes Kunz, manufacturer of the vehicle AK Rasant
c	Cost per unit (€/unit)
C	Total costs (€/year)
cf	Compare
CF	Cash flow
CSA	Citrogeot Société Anonyme, manufacturer of the vehicle CSA Chevalier
D	Demand
ed.	Edition
e.g.	For example
EL	Economic life
et al.	And others
EUR	Euro
FVA	Future value of an annuity
FVF	Future value factor
i	Interest rate or discount rate in % per period
i.e.	That is

Inv	Investment
IRR	Internal rate of return
max	Maximum
min	Minimum
MU	Monetary unit
n	Time, number of periods
NPV	Net present value
op. cit.	In the work quoted
P	Profit
$p(h_i)$	Probability for high demand in period i
$p(l_i)$	Probability for low demand in period i
$p(h_j/h_i)$	Probability for high demand in period j, if demand was high in period i
$p(l_j/h_i)$	Probability for low demand in period j, if demand was high in period i
$p(h_j/l_i)$	Probability for high demand in period j, if demand was low in period i
$p(l_j/l_i)$	Probability for low demand in period j, if demand was low in period i
PI	Profitability index
pp	Pages
PV	Present value
PVA	Present value of an annuity
PVF	Present value factor
q^n	Future value factor
q^{-n}	Present value factor

Abbreviations and Symbols

R	Accounting rate of return
resp.	Respective
SFF	Sinking fund factor
SM	Sayonara Motors Corporation, manufacturer of the vehicle SM Samurai
SV	Salvage value
SV_B	Salvage value at the beginning of the remaining economic life
SV_E	Salvage value at the end of the remaining economic life
t	Point in time, period
V_i	Value of a Cash Amount in period i
x	Activity quantity of an alternative
y	Years

1 An Introduction to the Investment Decision

1.1 Learning Objectives

This chapter will provide you with the basics of financial appraisal of investment projects.

- By means of a fictitious car sharing enterprise we will explain the requirements and the aims of investment appraisal as well as
- the interaction between investment decisions and business finance.
- It is necessary to identify different types of investment and
- to distinguish between the stages of the investment process.
- Furthermore, a first overview of investment appraisal techniques is provided.
- Finally, this chapter ends, as all the other chapters will do, with questions and respective solutions.

This book is based on a continuous case study that is introduced in the following section.

1.2 Case: Car Sharing Company

During a break between two classes a group of students have the idea to found a car sharing company. In so doing they aim to supplement their income and moreover to improve their quality of life. In order to help them transact business someone makes a used laptop and a printer at the amount of € 1,000 available to the group of students. Furthermore the students bring in € 20,000 that a bank lends them at a rate of 5 % interest on the merits of their undertaking. In this case study, the selection of the interest rate is expressly not geared to the reality, but is selected so that results can be easily and understandably recalculated.

The most urgent initial task to run the business is the purchase of an appropriate vehicle. Since the students can't be certain of the success of their business a rather inexpensive vehicle should be bought, because it could be resold easily in case of need. After a pre-selection there are two vehicles short-listed: The model AK Rasant of Archimedes Kunz Company and the model SM Samurai of Sayonara Motors Corporation.

With the help of the different methods of investment appraisal from Chapter 2 on, we will pursue the question of which vehicle should be purchased. In order to focus attention on areas of major importance we start working with a very simplified model. The real world complexities like uncertainty, taxation or capital scarcity are taken into account. They will be added layer by layer to the model with which we start. However, as a start, we begin with the basics of investment decisions.

1.3 Investment Decisions and Business Finance

Capital expenditure decisions involve a substantial outlay and will bring benefits over a long time horizon. An investment involves the sacrifice of an immediate level of consumption (i.e. a dividend now) in exchange for the expectation of an increase in future consumption (i.e. an enlarged dividend later). To be worthwhile the investment project's benefit must warrant its initial capital cost and some extra benefit to compensate for the risk involved. Decisions on investment projects have a direct impact on the ability of an organisation to meet its goals. For investment decision making, we usually use as a valuation base the fact whether the investment project benefits the shareholders.

A necessary precondition to undertake an investment is its financing. This means providing the funds to start and sustain the business. The main purpose of business finance is to assure the financial equilibrium to provide the necessary liquidity for the enterprise.[1] We are not concerned here with whether the funds that finance the investment project should be provided by financial markets outside the company or whether the funds are generated from the returns of the organisation itself. We assume that the company has adequate financial resources to undertake the investment, so that we can focus on the cash flow of the investment. In Chapter 5 we are going to drop this assumption. There you will learn how to integrate financing flows and how to deal with special features of financing.

---

[1] For the different financing alternatives see Gräfer, Horst, Rolf Beike and Guido A. Scheld, Finanzierung, 5th ed., Berlin 2001; Jahrmann, Fritz-Ulrich, Finanzierung, 5th ed., Herne/Berlin 2003 and Olfert, Klaus, and Christopher Reichel, Finanzierung, 13th ed., Ludwigshafen 2005.

1.4 Classification of Investments and Stages of the Investment Process

With regard to the nature of the asset we can distinguish between the following investments: Physical investment (e.g. real property or machinery), financial investment (e.g. stocks or shares in other companies) or intangible investment (e.g. investment in employee education, investment in advertising campaigns, research and development). On principle, investment appraisals can be made regardless of how the investments are classified.

According to the reason for the investment we distinguish between investments to found or to extend a business and reinvestments (replacement investments or rationalisation investment). In this book, for each method, we first address the problems which arise when comparing alternatives of asset purchase. We then cover the application of investment appraisal techniques to the replacement of an asset, in order to accommodate the different decision situations.

The decision-making process consists of different stages:

1. Planning.
2. Identifying the alternatives to be considered and their transformation into workable proposals.
3. Appraising the alternatives and selecting the best one with regard to the organisation's goals is the third step. In order to select an investment opportunity and to decide whether the firm is better off or not after implementing the investment, appraisal techniques are used. The basic question is whether the benefits of an investment are worth the outlay. This stage is considered in this book. But this is not yet the end of the decision-making process. After having decided which investment to undertake,
4. Implementing the decision.
5. The final stage entails reviewing the selected investment project.

1.5 Investment Appraisal Techniques

To undertake an investment appraisal exercise several techniques can be used. The role of investment appraisal is to ensure that relevant information is gathered relating to all the alternatives and to enable decisions to be taken with consideration being given to the objectives of the organisation. Whether we take into account that money and, therefore, the input variables of an investment appraisal have a time value or not, we distinguish between

- non-discounting methods of investment appraisal (Chapter 2) and
- discounting methods of investment appraisal (Chapter 3).

At this stage it is worth pointing out their most important characteristics in Table 1-1.

Table1-1 Characteristics of the methods of investment appraisal

Non-discounting methods	Discounting methods
• The values from the investment are represented through costs and revenues.	• The values from the investment are represented through cash inflow and cash outflow.
• The methods don't focus on the whole life of the project, that is, its useful economic life expectancy. They work with an average value of a representative period instead.	• Not only is the amount of money to be paid and received from the investment important to the investment decision, but also the point of time at which money is generated.
• The time value of money is not considered. Whether a payment is made at the beginning or at the end of the economic life of an asset is not taken into account. This is the reason for the name non-discounting methods.	• The times at which money is realised is considered. All cash flows received at different points of time are converted to a common reference point to allow direct comparison.

Investment decision making under conditions of uncertainty is presented in Chapter 4, advanced topics of investment appraisal are considered in Chapter 5.

All of the techniques to be discussed require the input of data relating to the investment project. The advice given by investment appraisal methods can only be as good as the data on which the calculations are based. Any fixed costs or other profits of an existing company will be the same regardless whether the investment is realised or not. They are not affected by the investment decision under appraisal. Relevant data is the marginal or incremental cash flow or profit attributable to the commencement of the new project and not the total cash flow or profit of the company. The role of investment appraisal is to ensure that appropriate information is gathered relating to the investment alternatives.

1.6 Summary and Evaluation

Decisions on capital investment are of great importance, because they account for a large portion of a firm's financial means. They are very costly or impossible to reverse and have an impact on the ability of an organisation to meet its goals. For all kinds of investments the stages of the investment process are similar. The selection of an investment is one of the stages of the capital budgeting process. It is made possible by the various appraisal techniques. The crucial question is whether the benefits from undertaking an investment are sufficient to warrant the initial outlay. After a broad distinction we differentiate between non-discounting methods and discounting methods of investment appraisal. They differ in how to deal with cash flow to be expended or received at different times.

1.7 Exercises with Answers

1.7.1 Exercises

Exercise 1-1 Connection between investment and financing

Assign the following business transactions to the right column:

Business transaction	Investment	Financing
A loan is taken out by the house bank.		
A new car is bought.		
An existing vehicle is replaced by a technically better one.		
The company ploughs back profits for future investments.		
An incorporated company takes in shares from new shareholders.		
The chief executive officer decides to invest in environmental measures.		

Exercise 1-2 Investment and financing with their performance in the balance sheet and the profit and loss account

Go back to Section 1.2, where the foundation of the car sharing company is described.

a) Develop the opening balance sheet for the car sharing company.

b) Suppose the purchase of a vehicle costing € 12,000 with an anticipated average life of 3 years. The whole payment is done in one step through the bank account. How does the opening balance sheet change?

c) After the first business year the first income for hiring the vehicle comes to the company's bank account: € 5,500. What is the balance sheet like after this first business year? You should also take into consideration that interest on liabilities has to be paid. To get a good overview perform the profit and loss account as well.

d) Money at the amount of the profit earned for the year is used to pay back loans. Please construct the respective balance sheet.

Exercise 1-3 Types of investments

Assign the following investments to the right column:

Investment	Physical investment	Financial investment	Intangible investment
You buy a cleaning machine.			
An extensive survey to explore consumers' habits is ordered.			
The company uses excess liquidity to buy stocks and bonds.			

Exercise 1-4 Investment appraisal

What is the most important difference between non-discounting and discounting methods of investment appraisal?

1.7.2 Answers

Answer to exercise 1-1 Connection between investment and financing

Business transaction	Investment	Financing
A loan is taken out by the house bank.		●
A new car is bought.	●	
An existing vehicle is replaced by a technically better one.	●	
The company ploughs back profits for future investments.		●
An incorporated company takes in shares from new shareholders.		●
The chief executive officer decides to invest in environmental measures.	●	

Answer to exercise 1-2 Investment and financing with their performance in the balance sheet and the profit and loss account

a)

Assets	Balance Sheet I		Liabilities and Equity
Cash	20,000	Liabilities	20,000
Equipment	1,000	Shareholders' equity	1,000
Total	21,000	Total	21,000

(All figures in Euros if not stated otherwise.)

b)

Assets	Balance Sheet II		Liabilities and Equity
Cash	8,000	Liabilities	20,000
Equipment	1,000	Shareholders' equity	1,000
Car pool	12,000		
Total	21,000	Total	21,000

c)

Expenses	Profit and Loss Account		Income
Depreciation	4,000	Sales	5,500
Interest	1,000		
Profit	500		
Total	5,500	Total	5,500

The amount of € 5,500 goes in full to the bank account. The shareholders' equity doesn't rise at this amount though, because after the first business year depreciation for the car has to be considered. The depreciation rate is € 12.000 ÷ 3 years = € 4.000. Furthermore, 5 % interest has to be paid on loans. The bank account goes down this amount.

Assets	Balance Sheet III		Liabilities and Equity
Cash	12,500	Liabilities	20,000
Equipment	1,000	Shareholders' equity	1,500
Car pool	8,000		
Total	21,500	Total	21,500

d)

Assets	Balance Sheet IV		Liabilities and Equity
Cash	12,000	Liabilities	19,500
Equipment	1,000	Shareholders' equity	1,500
Car pool	8,000		
Total	21,000	Total	21,000

Answer to exercise 1-3 Types of investments

Investment	Physical investment	Financial investment	Intangible investment
You buy a cleaning machine.	●		
An extensive survey to explore consumers' habits is ordered.			●
The company uses excess liquidity to buy stocks and bonds.		●	

Answer to exercise 1-4 Investment appraisal

Non-discounting methods are based on averages taken from a representative period. The elements of the calculation for the non-discounting methods are costs and revenues, with the exception of the payback period. Discounting methods, on the contrary, are based on transactions actually paid over time. Based on financial mathematics we consider the concrete point in time of cash inflow and cash outflow.

2 Non-discounting Methods of Investment Appraisal

2.1 Learning Objectives

After having been acquainted with the fundamentals of investment appraisal in the introductory chapter, in the following chapter you will get an overview of the non-discounting methods of investment appraisal. At the end of the chapter you will know,

- which ways exist to evaluate an investment project among the non-discounting methods of investment appraisal,
- the characteristics of these techniques and
- the strengths and weaknesses of each of these methods.
- Given the widespread use of non-discounting methods of investment appraisal it is necessary to have an understanding of each of these methods and of their shortcomings.
- For each method we address projects of two types: Asset expansion projects and asset replacement projects.
- The specifics that result from liquidity values at the end of the economic life of the asset are explained in a separate section for each method.
- If the utilisation of a durable investment good can be predicted only with difficulty, then it is useful to compute so-called critical values for the asset's workload.
- Questions and solutions will lead to the confidence which is necessary to understand the concepts of the non-discounting methods of investment appraisal.

2.2 Cost Comparison Method

2.2.1 Introduction

Within the cost comparison method we compare the costs of two or more alternative investment projects. All other factors influencing the alternatives remain unconsidered or are regarded as constant. They will be taken into account in other methods of investment appraisal, which are presented in later chapters.

We distinguish between two basically different applications of the non-discounting methods of investment appraisal.

1. Comparison of alternatives: We address the problem which arises when an asset is first bought.

2. Decision for replacement: In this case we calculate the optimal replacement time of an alternative which has already been realised. The classical situation here involves technical innovation. In principle, existing equipment can still be used, but new equipment would entail lower current maintenance costs. We have to scrutinise if it is profitable at all to replace the existing asset through a new one, and if so, when it would be most advantageous to do so.

While applying the cost comparison method we choose the alternative whose costs are the lowest. As decision criterion we choose either the total costs per period C (comparison of costs per period) or the cost per unit c (comparison of cost per unit). A comparison of the costs per unit is performed, if the quantity produced by the alternatives is not equal and, therefore, a look at the total costs per period would distort the results of the calculation. For a comparison of the costs per unit the total costs per year C have to be divided by the quantity produced x.

The decision criterion for the cost comparison method is: An investment project 1 is advantageous to an investment project 2, if its costs are lower. This means

- for a comparison of costs per period: $C_1 < C_2$ and

- for a comparison of cost per unit: $c_1 < c_2$.

In the following section we perform the cost comparison method for the case study from Chapter 1.2.

2.2.2 Comparison of Alternatives

We go back to the decision which has to be taken by the car sharing company. The initial capital cost of the AK Rasant are € 9,000, those of the SM Samurai € 14,000. Both vehicles have the same maximum capacity of 35,000 kilometres per year. The total capacity is actually used. While using the cars at their capacity limit, the anticipated average life is 2 years for the AK Rasant and 3 years for the SM Samurai. This is a rather cautious estimate, because it is difficult to predict how frequently changing drivers may burden the vehicles.

2.2 Cost Comparison Method

Taxes and insurance are the same for both vehicles: € 2,000 per year. With regard to the manufacturer's information, preventive maintenance should be lower for the car type SM Samurai. Average fixed costs for preventive maintenance are € 1,000 per year for the AK Rasant and € 800 per year for the SM Samurai. The valuation of average repair costs is € 1,500 per year for the AK Rasant and € 1,000 per year for the SM Samurai. Operating expenses are € 0.15 per kilometre for the AK Rasant and € 0.17 per kilometre for the SM Samurai.

We perform a comparison of alternatives. That is, we look at the average total cost per year, due to the fact that planned driving performance is equal for both vehicles.[2] Total costs per period are the result of two components, running costs and capital costs.

```
    Running costs (personnel, material, maintenance, energy etc.)
+   Capital costs (depreciation and interest)
=   Total costs
```

Whereas running costs can be derived directly from the information you find in the description of the case study, capital costs have to be calculated based on the purchase cost of the respective asset. Imputed depreciation is derived from the expenses for the particular asset.[3] Usually we act on the assumption that the company calculates depreciation on a straight-line basis.

$$\text{Imputed depreciation per period} = \frac{\text{initial outlay}}{\text{anticipated average life}}$$

This is the result for both vehicles:

$$\text{Depreciation type AK Rasant: } \frac{€\,9{,}000}{2 \text{ years}} = €\,4{,}500/\text{year}$$

$$\text{Depreciation type SM Samurai: } \frac{€\,14{,}000}{3 \text{ years}} = €\,4{,}667/\text{year}$$

---

[2] If the annual capacity were different, one would regard average cost per kilometre, which can be calculated by dividing annual total cost by the amount of kilometres driven.

[3] If one follows the principle of substantial maintenance of capital, imputed depreciation could be derived from the replacement costs as well.

Moreover, as part of the capital costs, imputed interest has to be considered. Interest has to be paid not only on liabilities but also on equity. If a company uses equity to finance its investments, then it misses the opportunity to use that capital for another investment leading to positive interest or income. These are so-called opportunity costs or costs from missed opportunities to earn interest or income. Within a comparison of costs, imputed interest is calculated with regard to the average capital invested.

While calculating the amount of imputed interest it is common practice to apply the so-called average method. In doing so the imputed interest rate is multiplied by the average capital employed.[4] Therefore, we act on the assumption that the amount of capital invested decreases at a constant rate over time and that the average capital employed equals half the initial outlay. If additional current assets are needed their value has to be added to the average capital employed. Assets that do not wear out over time are calculated with their total initial outlay.

$$\text{Imputed interest per period} = \frac{\text{initial outlay}}{2} \times \text{interest rate}$$

This method leads to constant amounts of interest per year over the useful life expectancy of the asset. What Figure 2-1 illustrates is that the application of the method of averages leads to an underestimation of the capital invested in the first half of the anticipated average life and to an overestimation of the capital invested in the second half. The marked areas show the mistakes made while applying the method of averages. If you compare the triangles you will easily understand that both have the same size. Thus, the mistakes made while imputing the simplifying average method will balance each other out over the entire useful economic life.

---

[4] Furthermore you can apply the so-called method of residual values. Then the imputed interest rate is multiplied by the residual values at the end of each year. This leads to declining amounts of interest over time. This is, of course, more complex with regard to the calculation of interest than the method of averages.

Figure 2-1 Average capital employed

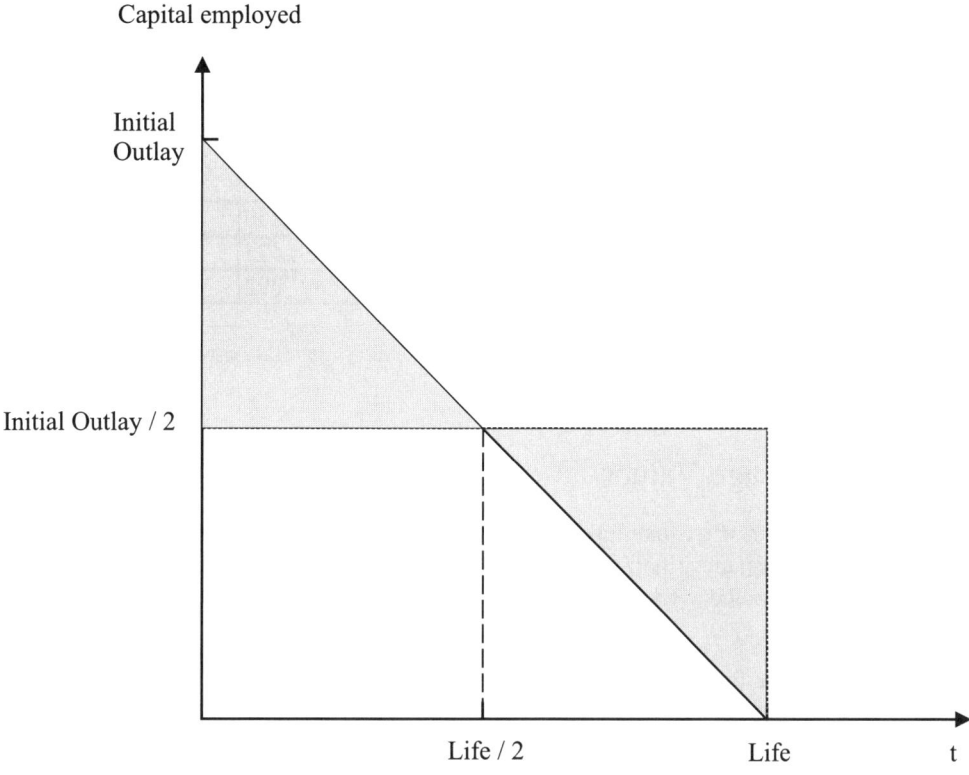

In our example we choose an interest rate of 5 %, due to the fact, that this is the interest rate at which the car sharing company borrowed its seed capital.[5] Thus:

Imputed interest type AK Rasant: $\dfrac{€\,9{,}000}{2} \times 0.05 = €\,225$/year

Imputed interest type SM Samurai: $\dfrac{€\,14{,}000}{2} \times 0.05 = €\,350$/year

Finally, running cost and capital cost must be added for both vehicles. Then a comparison is made in table form (Table 2-1).

---

[5] In practise, interest rates for equity on one side and for liabilities on the other side are usually weighed according to the gearing between equity and liabilities. See Ross, Stephen A., Randolph W. Westerfield and Bradford D. Jordan, Corporate Finance: Essentials, 5th ed., New York 2006, pp. 372-382.

Table 2-1 Comparison of alternatives by the cost comparison method

	AK Rasant	SM Samurai
Imputed depreciation	4,500	4,667
Imputed interest	225	350
Taxes and insurance	2,000	2,000
Maintenance	1,000	800
Repair	1,500	1,000
Operating expenses	5,250	5,950
Total costs	14,475	14,767
Difference between total costs		292

We see that one should buy model AK Rasant, because average total costs per year are lower by the amount of € 292.

2.2.3 Salvage Values

Our situation changes if we take into account that one could resell the vehicles at the end of their useful life expectancy. In this context we estimate the amount an asset can be sold for at the end of the anticipated average life. We assume:

- Salvage value for type AK Rasant: € 1,000
- Salvage value for type SM Samurai: € 2,000

Salvage values change both imputed depreciation and imputed interest rates. First, we look at the changed imputed depreciation per period. Only the capital exceeding the salvage value is subject to a diminution over the anticipated average life of the asset, because we will get back the whole salvage value at the end of the useful life expectancy.

$$\text{Imputed depreciation per period} = \frac{\text{initial outlay} - \text{salvage value}}{\text{anticipated average life}}$$

In our example we get:

$$\text{Model AK Rasant:} \quad \frac{€\,9{,}000 - €\,1{,}000}{2} = €\,4{,}000$$

$$\text{Model SM Samurai:} \quad \frac{€\,14{,}000 - €\,2{,}000}{3} = €\,4{,}000$$

2.2 Cost Comparison Method

When salvage values are considered, imputed interest per period also changes. The salvage value itself does not decline over time. It is fixed over the economic lifetime of the asset and thus has to be multiplied completely by the interest rate. Accordingly, the first summand for the calculation of the imputed interest rates is

$$\text{Salvage value} \times \text{interest rate}$$

But the capital beyond it (initial outlay – salvage value) has to be written off and hence sustains an annual diminution in value. The second summand is therefore:

$$\frac{\text{initial outlay - salvage value}}{2} \times \text{interest rate}$$

The addition of both components leads to the following:

$$\frac{\text{initial outlay - salvage value}}{2} \times \text{interest rate} + \text{salvage value} \times \text{interest rate}$$

$$= \left(\frac{\text{initial outlay - salvage value}}{2} + \text{salvage value} \right) \times \text{interest rate}$$

$$= \left(\frac{\text{initial outlay - salvage value} + 2 \times \text{salvage value}}{2} \right) \times \text{interest rate}$$

$$= \left(\frac{\text{initial outlay + salvage value}}{2} \right) \times \text{interest rate}$$

We sum up:

$$\boxed{\text{Imputed interest per period} = \left(\frac{\text{initial outlay + salvage value}}{2} \right) \times \text{interest rate}}$$

Now we use the data of our example:

for type AK Rasant: $\left(\frac{€\,9{,}000 + €\,1{,}000}{2} \right) \times 0.05 = €\,250$

for type SM Samurai: $\left(\frac{€\,14{,}000 + €\,2{,}000}{2} \right) \times 0.05 = €\,400$

Table 2-2 Comparison of alternatives by the cost comparison method with salvage values

	AK Rasant	SM Samurai
Imputed depreciation	4,000	4,000
Imputed Interest	250	400
Taxes and insurance	2,000	2,000
Maintenance	1,000	800
Repair	1,500	1,000
Operating expenses	5,250	5,950
Total costs	14,000	14,150
Difference between total costs	150	

From Table 2-2 we can see that the model type AK Rasant remains favourable. But the advantage in annual cost drops back from € 292 to € 150.

2.2.4 Critical Values

Up until now we assumed in our example that the activity quantity per period – here kilometres driven per year – is known. However, it isn't realistic that this exact quantity is known, because one cannot predict how many kilometres the vehicle will be driven in the respective period. In these cases we calculate the quantum which leads to equal costs for both alternatives. This is the so-called critical quantity. It can always be calculated if one of the alternatives has higher initial capital outlays and the other alternative has higher variable costs.

First we have to derive the cost functions for both alternatives. To reach this aim for either vehicle we take into account fixed costs and variable costs. The figures are repeated from the comparison of alternatives without salvage values (Table 2-1), and they are now represented in Table 2-3:

Table 2-3 Basic data for the calculation of critical values

	AK Rasant	SM Samurai
Fixed Costs	€ 9,225	€ 8,817
Variable Costs	€ 0.15	€ 0.17

Hence, we get the following cost functions:

$$C_{AK} = €\ 9{,}225 + x \times €\ 0.15$$

$$C_{SM} = €\ 8{,}817 + x \times €\ 0.17$$

2.2 Cost Comparison Method

Equating both cost functions yields the mathematical solution for the critical quantity:

$$€\,9{,}225 + x \times €\,0.15 = €\,8{,}817 + x \times €\,0.17$$
$$\Leftrightarrow \quad €\,408 = x \times €\,0.02$$
$$\Leftrightarrow \quad x = 20{,}400$$

This calculation can be proved by solving the cost functions for the computed value of 20,400 kilometres. Then we check whether the total costs for either function are equal.

$$C_{AK} = €\,9{,}225 + 20{,}400 \times €\,0.15 = €\,12{,}285$$
$$C_{SM} = €\,8{,}817 + 20{,}400 \times €\,0.17 = €\,12{,}285$$

This condition is fulfilled. If the number of kilometres driven is below 20,400 the vehicle type SM Samurai is favourable. If the number of kilometres driven is higher, then the vehicle type AK Rasant is better. Thus, the decision makers of the car sharing company must estimate whether the activity quantity will be higher or lower than the calculated critical quantity. Figure 2-2 summarises this information in graphical form.

Figure 2-2 Critical activity quantity by the cost comparison method

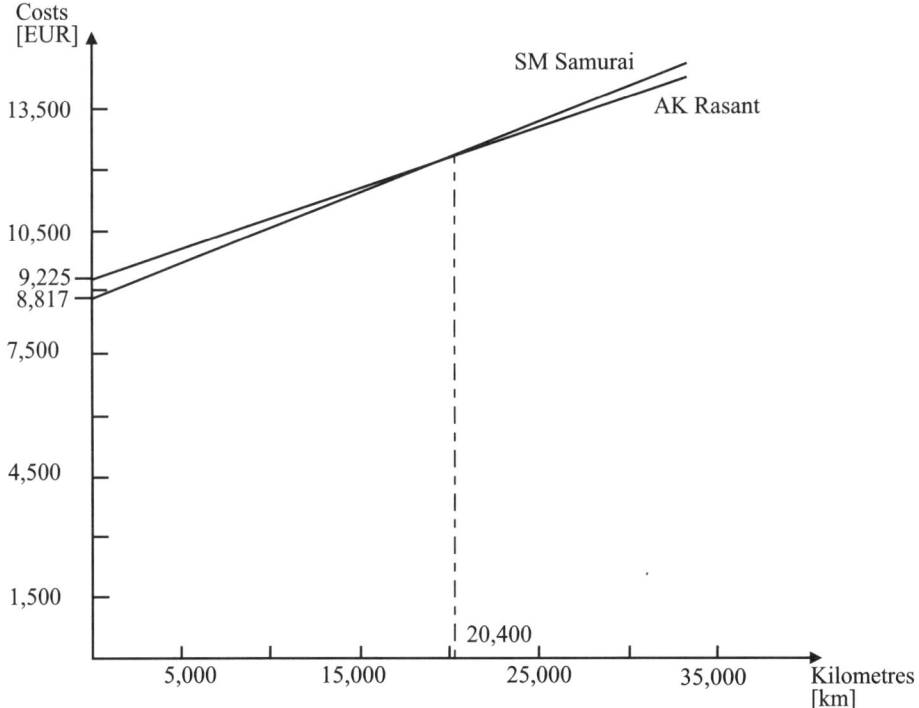

2.2.5 Replacement Decision

Existing projects ought to be constantly reviewed to ensure that they are still viable. When technical innovation is involved we have to decide whether it is more profitable to replace the existing asset with a more efficient asset or if it is more useful to keep the existing asset working. Of course, the replacement may be made due to marketing requirements rather than for technical reasons. For the replace decision we must determine what would be the optimal sale time for an asset currently in use. The first subtask is to determine whether it makes sense to replace the vehicle at all.

Therefore, we refer to our starting example. It is assumed that the AK Rasant has been bought. After one year of the two year economic life of the vehicle a replacement is considered. But for the moment we assume first that the existing vehicle cannot be sold. Table 2-4 reports the data from a CSA Chevalier of the Citrogeot Société Anonyme with identical driving performance which could be bought at a good price:

Table 2-4 Basic data for the new vehicle

	CSA Chevalier
Initial outlay	10,000
Economic life	4
Taxes and insurance	1,800
Maintenance	800
Repair	500
Running costs per km	0.12

We need to consider what costs would accrue if the existing car is still used. These costs have to be compared to those accruing if a new car is bought.

Table 2-5 Relevant costs with regard to the replacement decision

Utilisation of the old vehicle	Purchase of a new vehicle
Fixed costs old vehicle	Fixed costs old vehicle
Variable costs old vehicle	Fixed costs new vehicle
	Variable costs new vehicle

2.2 Cost Comparison Method

The fixed costs for the old vehicle accrue in either case. Therefore, we can simplify the calculation by reducing the comparison to the marked items in Table 2-5. That is, we compare the variable costs of the existing car to the total costs of the new car.

> The decision criterion for the replacement decision is: An existing asset should be replaced by a new one if the relevant cost of the new asset is lower than the relevant cost of the old asset. This means
>
> - for a comparison of costs per period: $C_{new} < C_{old}$ and
> - for a comparison of cost per unit: $c_{new} < c_{old}$.

Now we carry out the cost comparison for the two alternatives described above.

Table 2-6 Replacement decision by the cost comparison method

	AK Rasant	CSA Chevalier
Imputed depreciation	0	2,500
Imputed interest	0	250
Taxes and insurance	2,000	1,800
Maintenance	1,000	800
Repair	1,500	500
Operating expenses	5,250	4,200
Total costs	9,750	10,050
Difference between total costs	300	

From the scheme of data in Table 2-6 we can see that the car type CSA Chevalier is cheaper with regard to current maintenance. But this effect does not compensate for the new fixed costs, depreciation and interest. Therefore, the advantage in total costs of € 300 of the AK Rasant means that the replacement is not useful.

With regard to the replacement decision salvage values must be considered, too. As with the comparison of alternatives, this is done by changing imputed depreciation and imputed interest respectively.

If we want to find the point – in terms of kilometres driven – at which is begins to be worth it to replace the vehicle, then we are asking for what may be called the critical performance factor. To calculate this critical value we equate:

Costs of the old vehicle which are relevant for the decision = Costs of the new vehicle which are relevant for the decision

$$€ 4{,}500 + x \times € 0.15 = € 5{,}850 + x \times € 0.12$$

$$\Leftrightarrow € 4{,}500 + x \times € 0.03 = € 5{,}850$$

$$\Leftrightarrow x \times € 0.03 = € 1{,}350$$

$$\Leftrightarrow x = 45{,}000$$

Thus both vehicles are equal if the annual mileage is 45,000 kilometres. The calculated driving performance can be checked easily by repeating the comparison of cost for exactly this number of kilometres:

Table 2-7 Check for the replacement decision by the cost comparison method

	AK Rasant	CSA Chevalier
Imputed depreciation	0	2,500
Imputed interest	0	250
Taxes and insurance	2,000	1,800
Maintenance	1,000	800
Repair	1,500	500
Operating expenses	6,750	5,400
Total costs	11,250	11,250

The check made in Table 2-7 shows that an annual mileage of 45,000 kilometres leads to identical total costs. Not until the mileage exceeds 45,000 kilometres per year, would the replacement be preferable.

Finally, we have to determine the optimal time for an existing asset to be replaced by a new one. For this reason salvage values of the old asset have to be considered. In our case this might be done not only by comparing the CSA Chevalier with the AK Rasant but furthermore by taking into account that the AK Rasant could be sold after the first period for € 2,000. However, at the end of the second period, which is the end of the vehicle's economic life no further salvage value exists.

At the beginning of year 2, at which point the decision should be made, only the salvage value represents the capital employed. The assumptions about the depreciation were made at the beginning of the economic life. They are no longer applicable for the changed data. Instead of the depreciation we calculate a reduction of the salvage value as follows. We calculate the difference between the salvage value at the beginning and at the end of the remaining economic life. This is divided by the remaining economic life.

2.2 Cost Comparison Method

$$\text{Reduction of the salvage value per period} = \frac{SV_B - SV_E}{\text{remaining economic life}}$$

Substituting in the known values gives

$$= \frac{€\,2{,}000 - €\,0}{1} = \frac{€\,2{,}000}{1} = €\,2{,}000$$

The calculation of the imputed interest is done by using the following equation:

$$\text{Imputed interest per period} = \left(\frac{SV_B + SV_E}{2}\right) \times \text{Interest rate}$$

Using the variables from the example the imputed interest per period is:

$$= \left(\frac{€\,2{,}000 + €\,0}{2}\right) \times 0.05$$

$$= €\,1{,}000 \times 0.05$$

$$= €\,50$$

Table 2-8 Replacement decision by the cost comparison method with salvage values

	AK Rasant	CSA Chevalier
Imputed depreciation	0	2,500
Imputed interest	50	250
Reduction of the liquidation value	2,000	0
Taxes and insurance	2,000	1,800
Maintenance	1,000	800
Repair	1,500	500
Operating expenses	5,250	4,200
Total costs	11,800	10,050
Difference between total costs		1,750

As shown in Table 2-8 the cost advantage of the replacement would be € 1,750. This results from the fact that the reduction of salvage values has to be considered for the existing car. This can be clearly understood because the more money we generate from the old asset, the sooner this project can be abandoned and the sooner the replacement is profitable.

2.2.6 Evaluation of the Cost Comparison Method

If a special approach of the non-discounting methods of investment appraisal should be assessed, then one has to be conscious of the overall assessment of all the non-discounting methods of investment appraisal. This will be presented in Chapter 2.6.

In the following, the advantages and disadvantages of the cost comparison method beyond this are summarised:

1. Only alternatives are compared, so we can not judge whether the investment is favourable at all. This way we minimise costs, but it might be possible that both alternatives are absolutely disadvantageous. In our case we compared the acquisition of two vehicles. If the business worked out badly then it would be potentially better to buy no car at all.

2. The cost comparison method is useful, if the investment alternatives have equal returns, initial outlays and lives. This might be the case for rather small replacement investments or rationalisation investments because then it can make sense to assume constant revenues and nearly unchanged variable costs of the alternatives.

3. We must check very carefully if a comparison of alternatives or a replacement decision is made, to be certain that we know for sure whether depreciation and interest have to be considered.

4. In practice, splitting costs into fixed and variable components can not always be done without reservation. It follows that it is often problematic to construct cost functions.

5. An investment is assessed only according to the accruing costs. Differences in quality that lead to different revenues remain unconsidered. These are taken into consideration with the following profit comparison method.

2.3 Profit Comparison Method

2.3.1 Introduction

So far our analysis focused on the costs of an investment. In the following, we extend the cost comparison method by the revenues from an investment. The students expect that they can earn different sales prices for the usage of the vehicles. After a carefully made estimate the AK Rasant generated revenues of € 0.49 per kilometre driven. With regard to the SM Samurai they are somehow more optimistic due to the better equipment and, therefore, estimate revenues of € 0.51 per kilometre driven.

2.3 Profit Comparison Method

Now, with the help of this additional data, a profit comparison should be performed. The decision criterion for the profit comparison method is the annual average profit.

> The decision criteria for the profit comparison method are:
> - A single investment is accepted, if its average expected profit is positive. This means: $P > 0$.
> - In the context of mutually exclusive investments, an investment project 1 is advantageous to an investment project 2 if its profit is larger. This means: $P_1 > P_2$.

In contrast to the cost comparison method, we must keep in mind when employing the profit comparison method, that profit per period rather than profit per unit must be considered for quantitatively unequal performance of the alternatives. The profit per unit is not significant. Hence, the period's total profit should be maximised.

2.3.2 Comparison of Alternatives

The average annual profit is calculated by subtracting the average annual costs from the average annual revenues.

> Average annual profit = Annual sales revenues – annual costs

The costs per period are taken from the cost comparison method (Table 2-1). Here they are repeated as Table 2-9 for convenience.

Table 2-9 Comparison of alternatives by the profit comparison method

	AK Rasant	SM Samurai
Sales revenues	17,150	17,850
- Total costs	14,475	14,767
= Annual profit	2,675	3,083
Difference in annual profit		408

The SM Samurai generates an annual average profit which exceeds that of the AK Rasant by € 408 and is accordingly preferable.

2.3.3 Salvage Values

As with the cost comparison method, salvage values change depreciation and interest. As a consequence, the means used in the cost comparison method are still appropriate. For this reason we transfer total costs from Table 2-2 and list them again in Table 2-10.

Table 2-10 Comparison of alternatives by the profit comparison method with salvage values

	AK Rasant	SM Samurai
Sales revenues	17,150	17,850
- Total costs	14,000	14,150
= Annual profit	3,150	3,700
Difference in annual profit		550

The SM Samurai generates an annual average profit which exceeds that of the AK Rasant by € 550 and is accordingly preferable.

2.3.4 Critical Values

If we assume that we do not know how many users can be found for the car and hence how many kilometres can be sold, then the critical value can be computed with the aid of the profit comparison method. Equating both the profit functions yields the critical mileage. Again we refer to the data from the comparison of alternatives without salvage values (Table 2-3).

$$P_{AK} = x \times (€\,0.49 - €\,0.15) - €\,9{,}225 = x \times €\,0.34 - €\,9{,}225$$

$$P_{SM} = x \times (€\,0.51 - €\,0.17) - €\,8{,}817 = x \times €\,0.34 - €\,8{,}817$$

We can see that both the profit functions do not intersect. They are parallel. The vehicle type SM Samurai is always preferable due to its lower fixed costs. In spite of that an example where both the profit functions do intersect can be found in exercise 2-6.

2.3.5 Replacement Decision

To decide whether it is profitable to replace an existing asset by a new one within the cost comparison method we compared the variable costs of the new asset with the sum of fixed and variable costs of the new asset. This consideration is further developed by the profit comparison method as follows:

2.3 Profit Comparison Method

> The decision criterion for the replacement decision is: An existing asset should be replaced through a new one if the profit after replacement is larger than before.
> This means: $P_{new} > P_{old}$.

If the replacement of the existing asset leads to incremental profit, then it is always worthwhile to perform the replacement. We refer to the data from the replacement decision by the cost comparison method (Table 2-6) and consider moreover that the sales price for one kilometre of the CSA Chevalier is supposed to be € 0.55. From Table 2-11 you can get the results.

Table 2-11 Decision about the replacement of the AK Rasant by the profit comparison method

	AK Rasant	CSA Chevalier
Sales revenues	17,150	19,250
- Total costs	9,750	10,050
= Annual profit	7,400	9,200
Difference in annual profit		1,800

Consequently the replacement should be made, because the annual average profit will exceed that of the old vehicle retained by € 1,800.

Preceding the purchase of the SM Samurai, the decision on the replacement should be based on the data in Table 2-12. The total costs of the SM Samurai are computed according to Table 2-1 by adding the costs for taxes, insurance, maintenance, repair and operating expenses for 35,000 kilometres.

Table 2-12 Decision about the replacement of the SM Samurai by the profit comparison method

	SM Samurai	CSA Chevalier
Sales revenues	17,850	19,250
- Total costs	9,750	10,050
= Annual profit	8,100	9,200
Difference in annual profit		1,100

It follows that the replacement would be worthwhile also because the average annual profit will exceed that of the old vehicle retained by € 1,100.

2.3.6 Evaluation of the Profit Comparison Method

1. The profit comparison method allows for considering the investment's revenues. If the investment alternatives lead to different revenues then it is useful to perform a profit comparison approach instead of a cost comparison approach. This is generally the case with asset expansion investments.

2. Furthermore, the profit comparison method allows individual project evaluation. In that case the decision criterion is: $P > 0$.

3. In practise it is problematic to assign concrete revenues to a special investment.

4. Another shortcoming associated with the accounting profit method is the calculation of average values. If, for example, high repair costs occur in the last year of the economic life, it might be useful to sell the asset earlier. The longer the economic life of the investment and the bigger the investment, the more imprecise results become from the generation of average values.

5. A reasonable decision taken employing the profit comparison method requires identical initial outlays and identical economic lives. Here is an example:

Investment A	Investment B
Initial outlay € 100,000	Initial outlay € 110,000
Economic life: 4 years	Economic life: 3 years
Average annual profit € 5,000	Average annual profit € 6,000

Now a decision in favour of investment B based solely on the average annual profit would not be automatically correct because, if an investor with a seed capital of € 110,000 instead selected investment A, he could invest the difference of € 10,000 elsewhere. This might generate an additional profit. The profits added from both investments might be greater than € 6,000 per year. Finally, it is difficult to calculate average values if the economic life is unequal and if the investments with the shorter economic life cannot be generally replaced. In that case, the profit of € 6,000 could not be generated without any problem in year 4, either.

6. The superiority of an investment is based solely on emerging profit. So far, the capital employed to generate these profits remains unconsidered. In the following accounting rate of return method it is taken into account.

2.4 Accounting Rate of Return Method

2.4.1 Introduction

To generate profit is always the principal aim of a company. But it makes a difference whether a profit of € 10 is made with an investment of € 5 or with an investment of € 100. For this reason the average profit per period is put in relation to the average capital employed that generated the respective profit.[6]

$$\text{Accounting rate of return} = \frac{\text{Average annual profit}}{\text{Average capital employed}} \times 100$$

The investment's average rate of return per period shows the rate of return on the money invested. This can be compared with the investment of a certain amount of money on deposit. In that case interest gained is also compared to the seed capital. Hence, the rate of return is a ratio which regards some measure of profit in relation to some measure of variable causation.

The decision criteria for the accounting rate of return method are:

- A single investment is accepted, if its return on capital employed exceeds the minimum acceptable level of return on capital employed. This means: $R > R_{min}$.
- In the context of mutually exclusive investments, an investment project 1 is advantageous to an investment project 2, if its return on capital employed is higher. This means: $R_1 > R_2$.

2.4.2 Comparison of Alternatives

The starting point of the calculation is the incremental annual profit generated by an investment project. It can be taken from a previous profit comparison method or it can be newly derived for this purpose. The profit from the profit comparison method has to be corrected by imputed interest, because interest has been deducted by calculating the average annual profit. This correction is necessary because the accounting rate of return aims at the return of the capital invested. If interest were not subtracted then only the return in excess of the interest already considered would be computed, but not the average return on capital employed.

---

[6] We could, of course, divide the profit instead of the average capital employed by the total capital outlay at the beginning of the investment. Then this should be done equally for all investment alternatives to ensure that the results can be compared. Cf. Kruschwitz, Lutz, Investitionsrechnung, 10th ed., München 2005, p. 36.

If one starts instead from the revenues generated from the investment, then depreciation and variable costs must be deducted to get the average annual profit.

Table 2-13 Comparison of alternatives by the accounting rate of return method

	AK Rasant	SM Samurai
Profit after interest (from table 2-9)	2,675	3,083
+ Imputed interest (from table 2-1)	225	350
= Profit before interest	2,900	3,433
Average capital employed	4,500	7,000
Accounting rate of return in %	64.4	49.0

From Table 2-13 we deduce that the investment with the higher accounting rate of return should be preferred, hence the car type Rasant.

2.4.3 Salvage Values

If salvage values occur we must correct the annual depreciation and the average capital employed. These considerations come from Chapter 2.2.3 where we discussed the implications of salvage values within the cost comparison method.

$$\text{Average capital employed} = \frac{\text{Initial cost of the investment} + \text{salvage value}}{2}$$

This means we take the data from the profit comparison method with salvage values. Again we augment the average annual profit by the imputed interest.

Table 2-14 Comparison of alternatives by the accounting rate of return method with salvage values

	AK Rasant	SM Samurai
Profit after interest (from Table 2-10)	3,150	3,700
+ Imputed interest (from Table 2-2)	250	400
= Profit before interest	3,400	4,100
Average capital employed	5,000	8,000
Accounting rate of return in %	68.0	51.3

By referring to Table 2-14, the AK Rasant is still found favourable even considering salvage values. We realise that the rates of return are now slightly above those without salvage values. This was to be expected, because salvage values are favourable for the investor.

2.4.4 Replacement Decision

Even with the accounting rate of return method we can determine the optimal replacement point in time for an existing asset. For asset replacement investments or investments for rationalisation purposes we must ask for the saving of costs by the new asset with regard to the capital employed for it. For asset expansion projects the revenues usually change, too. Then we compare the increase of profits in relation to the capital employed. As regards content there is no difference between these two approaches because cost savings lead directly to higher profits.

The following value must be considered:

$$R = \frac{\text{average annual increase in profit}}{\text{average capital employed}} \times 100$$

Again we refer to the example within the profit comparison method because this allows emphasising the differences between the methods. The results are given in Table 2-15.

Table 2-15 Replacement decision by the accounting rate of return method

	AK Rasant	CSA Chevalier
Imputed depreciation	0	2,500
Imputed interest	0	250
Taxes and insurance	2,000	1,800
Maintenance	1,000	800
Repair	1,500	500
Operating expenses	5,250	4,200
Total costs	9,750	10,050
Revenues	17,150	19,250
Profit after interest	7,400	9,200
Profit before interest		9,450
Difference in profit		2,050

We get: $R = \frac{€\,2{,}050}{€\,5{,}000} \times 100 = 41\,\%$

This value must be compared to the minimum acceptable rate of return or to the rate of return from another investment.

2.4.5 Evaluation of the Accounting Rate of Return Method

1. The accounting rate of return method has the advantage over the cost comparison method in that it permits evaluation of the project on the basis of a percentage rate of return. A single investment can be assessed easily.

2. The result can be directly compared to the rate of return of an alternative investment project or to the company's target accounting return on investment. Evaluating the project on the basis of a percentage rate of return is familiar to all management.

3. The model is consistent with the numerous management reward systems that focus on accounting return on investment. Managers usually are concerned about the accounting profit they report to their shareholders.

4. The accounting rate of return is not a reliable measure because the average capital employed can be calculated differently and, therefore, the calculated rate of returns can differ.

5. The accounting rate of return method is advantageous to the profit method when the investment projects to be compared have different initial outlays.

6. If the initial outlays of the regarded investment alternatives are not identical, then the calculation has the implicit assumption that the so-called difference investment yields the rate of return of the inferior alternative. The following example illustrates the approach:

	Alternative A	Alternative B
Average capital employed	€ 20,000	€ 30,000
Rate of return	10 %	15 %

If from these data we conclude that alternative B represents the better investment, then we assume that the difference investment of € 10,000 yields a rate of return of 10 %, too. However, this is not likely to occur in practice.

2.5 Payback Method

2.5.1 Introduction

Finally, we can decide whether an investment opportunity is worth undertaking or not by considering the length of time it takes a project to recover its initial outlay.

$$\text{Payback period} = \frac{\text{Inital outlay}}{\text{average annual cash flow}}$$

One poses the following question: "How long does it take for an investment expenditure to pay for itself?" This means, we look for the length of time taken to recoup the initial outlay from the streams of revenue generated as a result of investment opportunities. The logic behind this approach is that the faster a project achieves payback, the less risky that project is. An investment project is, therefore, less favourable the longer it takes to pay back.

The decision criteria for the payback method are:
- A single investment is accepted, if it pays back the initial investment outlay within a certain predetermined time. This means: $t < t_{max}$.
- In the context of mutually exclusive investments, the projects can be ranked in terms of speed of payback. An investment project 1 is advantageous to an investment project 2, if it pays back quicker. This means: $t_1 < t_2$.

Alternatively we can calculate the payback period by cumulative cash flows. They are summed up until the added cash flows exceed the initial capital investment. This calculation would always be reasonable if the cash flows were highly fluctuating within the single years of the economic life because there the calculation of averages would lead to biased results.

2.5.2 Comparison of Alternatives

Average annual cash flow can be calculated by either of two methods. We can compare the difference between average annual cash inflow and average annual cash outflow. This is done in Table 2-16:

Table 2-16 Calculation of non-discounting payback through average annual cash flow

	AK Rasant	SM Samurai
Cash inflow	17,150	17,850
- Cash outflow	9,750	9,750
= Cash flow	7,400	8,100
Initial outlay	9,000	14,000
Payback in years	1.2	1.7

If we assume a profit comparison as in Table 2-9, which is based on the variables 'costs' and 'revenues', then we must add the annual depreciation and the imputed interest to the profit. They have been deducted in the profit comparison approach and must, therefore, be added to end up with an accurate measure of cash flow. Depreciation represents an allocation of the initial outlay over a number of periods. It is not a cash outflow. Likewise imputed interest does not lead to cash outflow. Therefore, the profit must be augmented by these positions if taken as the basis for the calculation of the cash flow.[7]

	Average annual profit
+	Imputed depreciation
+	Imputed interest
=	Average annual cash flow

Table 2-17 Calculation of non-discounting payback through average annual profit

	AK Rasant	SM Samurai
Average annual profit	2,675	3,083
+ Imputed depreciation	4,500	4,667
+ Imputed interest	225	350
= Cash flow	7,400	8,100
Initial outlay	9,000	14,000
Payback in years	1.2	1.7

Table 2-17 shows that both methods lead to the same result. In both cases we assume that cash flows are spread evenly over the year. Payback stresses the superiority of the AK Rasant.

---

[7] In practice it is often not possible to state whether an investment was financed with equity or debt. Accordingly, it is possible to regard the total interest as debit interest and therefore as costs that lead to cash outflows. In that case the profit should be augmented only by the imputed depreciation to end with the cash flow. Cf. e.g. Olfert, Klaus, and Christopher Reichel, Investition, 10th ed., Ludwigshafen 2006, p. 189.

2.5.3 Salvage Values

The initial outlay is reduced by the salvage value, because this amount of money need not be repaid.

$$\text{Payback period} = \frac{\text{Initial outlay} - \text{salvage value}}{\text{average annual cash flow}}$$

Then the payback period is calculated as in Table 2-18 either directly over the difference of cash inflow and cash outflow.

Table 2-18 Calculation of non-discounting payback through average annual cash flow with salvage values

	AK Rasant	SM Samurai
Initial outlay - salvage value	8,000	12,000
Cash inflow	17,150	17,850
Cash outflow	9,750	9,750
Cash flow	7,400	8,100
Payback in years	1.1	1.5

Or we start as in Table 2-19 with the average annual profit.

Table 2-19 Calculation of non-discounting payback through average annual profit with salvage values

	AK Rasant	SM Samurai
Average annual profit	3,150	3,700
+ Imputed depreciation	4,000	4,000
+ Imputed interest	250	400
= Cash flow	7,400	8,100
Initial outlay	8,000	12,000
Payback in years	1.1	1.5

The superiority of the AK Rasant can be identified by the shorter payback period. Besides we see that salvage values lead to faster payback.

2.5.4 Replacement Decision

If the payback period of an asset replacement investment or an asset expansion investment is determined, then the additional capital outlay is set in relation to the savings of cost or the incremental profit from the investment. We add depreciation and imputed interest exceeding debit interest of the new investment because they do not lead to a cash outflow.

$$\text{Payback period} = \frac{\text{Initial outlay of the new investment}}{\text{average incremental profit} + \text{depreciation of the new investment} + \text{imputed interest of the new investment}}$$

Table 2-20 shows the values on which the calculation of the payback period is based:

Table 2-20 Replacement decision by the non-discounting payback

	AK Rasant	CSA Chevalier
Imputed depreciation	0	2,500
Imputed interest	0	250
Taxes and insurance	2,000	1,800
Maintenance	1,000	800
Repair	1,500	500
Operating expenses	5,250	4,200
Total costs	9,750	10,050
Receipts	17,150	19,250
Annual profit	7,400	9,200
Difference in profit		1,800

Using these data to calculate the payback period yields

$$\frac{€10{,}000}{€1{,}800 + €2{,}500 + €250} = \frac{€10{,}000}{€4{,}550} = 2.2 \text{ years.}$$

2.5.5 Evaluation of the Payback Method

1. As a rule of thumb, the payback period is quickly and easily calculated, but it is difficult to establish the decision criterion 'acceptable payback period'. There is no objective measure of what constitutes an acceptable payback time.

2. It can be regarded as an additional calculation to the other methods of investment appraisal. It may allow appraising the risk of the investment by a measurement of the length of time it takes the receipts from an investment to pay back the invested capital cost.

3. The method does not take account of the cash flow which arise outside the payback period. The development of the investment project after the payback point of time is ignored. Payback period and accounting rate of return can lead to contradictory results. That is, despite a short payback period an investment may lead to a low rate of return and vice versa.

4. The payback period rule is biased towards liquidity and against long-term projects such as new products or research and development. This might be useful when capital rationing makes early recoupment of capital important.

2.6 Summary and Evaluation of the Non-Discounting Methods

After completing the non-discounting methods we summarise the decision criteria along with the investment advice for the comparison of alternatives without salvage values in Table 2-21:

Table 2-21 Results from the non-discounting methods of investment appraisal

Non-discounting Method	Decision Criterion	Accept
Cost comparison method	Average annual costs	AK Rasant
Profit comparison method	Average annual profit	SM Samurai
Accounting rate of return method	Rate of return in %	AK Rasant
Payback method	Payback time in years	AK Rasant

As the measures present conflicting judgements on the choice of investment, we have to check the suitability of different project evaluation techniques. Without any doubt it is not useful to simply count and choose the most frequently listed investment. In order to make the best decision regarding acceptance or rejection of an investment we must make use of the most appropriate method.

This is the accounting rate of return method. In case of doubt the decision should be based on this method, because it takes into account the capital employed. A sole consideration of profits is not reasonable because generated profits must be seen in relation to the capital invested. Payback allows for considering risk but it is not recommended as a criterion for accepting or rejecting projects. It may be useful as a support measure to other approaches.

The non-discounting methods of investment appraisal are finally evaluated as follows:

1. Non-discounting methods of investment appraisal can easily be implemented.

2. The data can readily be collected, because most necessary data is established within the cost accounting already.

3. According to the preconditions we use the cost comparison method, the profit comparison method or the accounting rate of return method. The payback period provides supplementary information.

4. Non-discounting methods are based on annual average values of costs and revenues and not on cash flow. Their conclusions cannot be expected to be more than approximations. They can be useful however, in getting a quick general assessment in particular cases. They provide a 'rule of thumb' check mechanism for the minor, short-lived investment projects.

5. Non-discounting approaches are straightforward, because they do not make high demands on the decision makers' mathematical expertise. This is an advantage in an economy based on division of labour in which people with different educations and vocational training work and decide together.

6. Their major drawback of not taking into account the time value of money is not compensated for by the consideration of imputed interest. Payments of equal amounts have different values depending upon when they occur. This drawback is eliminated by use of the discounting methods, which are now presented in Chapter 3.

2.7 Exercises with Answers

2.7.1 Exercises

Exercise 2-1 Cost comparison method – Comparison of alternatives

A company is considering buying a punching machine. Two possible systems are under investigation. They are characterised by the following data:

	Brand A	Brand B
Initial outlay	€ 30,000	€ 25,000
Fixed costs per year	€ 1,500	€ 1,200
Variable costs per punching process	€ 0.30	€ 0.32
Number of possible punching acts pro year	40,000	45,000
Life	10 years	10 years
Interest rate	8.0 %	8.0 %

Assess the investment with the help of the cost comparison method.

Exercise 2-2 Cost comparison method – Comparison of alternatives with salvage values

A company is undertaking an investment appraisal for a new copy machine. It estimates the relevant decision data of the alternatives to be as in the table:

	Copy machine A	Copy machine B
Initial outlay	€ 10,000	€ 20,000
Maintenance costs per year	€ 2,000	€ 500
Costs per copy	€ 0.05	€ 0.03
Amount of copies per year	10,000	10,000
Economic life	5 years	5 years
Interest rate	7.5 %	7.5 %

a) Evaluate the purchase of the respective copy machine using the cost comparison method. To start with, ignore salvage values.

b) Consider further that the used copy machines can be sold at the end of their useful life:

- Salvage value copy machine A: € 500
- Salvage value copy machine B: € 5,000

Exercise 2-3 Cost comparison method – Comparison of alternatives with critical values

A company is considering launching a new product. To produce this product a machine is necessary. The company must choose between two methods of production. The company uses an interest rate of 5 %. The financial details of both alternatives are as follows:

	Alternative I	Alternative II
Initial outlay in €	800,000	1,000,000
Economic life in years	8	8
Annual capacity in units	6,500	7,000
Variable production cost in € per unit	150	130
Other costs in € per year	60,000	70,000
Personell costs in € per year	210,000	240,000
Sales price in € per unit	220	220

Based on the cost comparison method, calculate when both alternatives are equal. Interpret the calculated value: At which level of unit production is the acquisition of which machine desirable? Check your result.

Exercise 2-4 Cost comparison method – Replacement decision

You should decide whether it is profitable to replace an old car by a new one. The original car can be abandoned if it has high maintenance costs. The current annual repair costs for the existing car are € 15,000 €. The following data is available for the new vehicle:

Initial outlay	€ 48,000
Economic life	8 years
Variable costs: Maintenance per year	€ 1,000
Interest rate	5 %

2.7 Exercises with Answers

Based on the cost comparison method, decide whether the asset should be replaced. Fixed costs for taxes and insurance are the same for the old and the new vehicle: € 1,500. Both vehicles require operating costs of € 0.20 per kilometre when driven 30,000 kilometres per year.

Exercise 2-5 Profit comparison method – Comparison of alternatives

Harvesting asparagus means working by hand. However, this may soon change. Recently, a harvesting machine has been developed for the vegetable growing on dams and has been presented at an agricultural fair. A manufacturer is willing to mass-produce it. The machine strains the entire asparagus dam, sorts out the asparagus and rebuilds the dam. Purchasing such a machine makes the employment of seasonal workers obsolete. Each year asparagus with a value of € 100,000 is produced.

The asparagus farmer is sceptical: "Asparagus stalks do not all grow at an equal rate. Whereas traditional harvesting cuts only asparagus longer than 8 inches, the machine also takes out the shorter plants."

The main financial details are shown in the table:

	Traditional harvesting	Harvesting machine
Initial outlay in €		144,000
Economic life of the machine in years		6
Percentage of utilisable asperagus	100	80
Annual maintenance of the harvesting machine		3,680
Personell costs seasonal workers per year	65,000	

A alternative investment on the farm for a milking machine would generate average annual profits of € 14,000. The farmer uses the profit comparison method to decide between those two investment opportunities. He can leave money on deposit at 6 %.

Exercise 2-6 Profit comparison method – Comparison of alternatives with critical values

In order to support its tourism offerings in the summer, a local authority runs an excursion boat which is need of renovation. There are two alternative offers for a new boat:

	Model A	Model B
Initial outlay	€ 850,000	€ 1,000,000
Economic life	10 years	10 years
Diverse fixed costs per year	€ 20,000	€ 20,000
Price for a one-way ticket	€ 4.80	€ 5.00
Variable costs per one-way ticket	€ 1.00	€ 0.90
Estimated amount of users per year	70,000 people	70,000 people

a) Using the profit comparison method, indicate which model the local authority should accept. (Interest rate 5 %)

b) When are both alternatives equal on the basis of the profit comparison method? Interpret the calculated value: At what number of users is which model boat preferable?

c) Check your result obtained in subtask b.

Exercise 2-7 Profit comparison method – Replacement decision

The Copy Inc. produces copy machines, which are sold at a unit price of € 6,000. The company has the opportunity to buy a new production line. For investment decisions the company implements a 13 % discount rate. The situation can be characterised by the following data:

	Old production line	New production line
Initial outlay	€ 25,000,000	€ 30,000,000
Maintenance per period	€ 5,000,000	€ 500,000
Economic life	10 years	10 years
Variable Costs per unit produced	€ 4,000	€ 3,900
Capacity per line	10,000 units	11,000 units

The company's marketing department estimates that the maximum capacity viable in each case could be marketable.

Is the replacement desirable according to the decision rule of the profit comparison method?

2.7 Exercises with Answers

Exercise 2-8 Accounting rate of return method – Comparison of alternatives

A local authority plans to purchase a new climbing wall for a gym used by several sports clubs. The clubs rent the gym for € 48 per hour. The local authority considers installing a new climbing wall and then raising the price to € 50 per hour.

The gym is rented 150 hours a month on average. The climbing wall costs € 15,000, and an economic life of 10 years is estimated. Moreover, special wood care is necessary and costs € 175 annually. The city council requires a rate of return for capital invested of 4 %.

What is the accounting rate of return of the investment, and what is your investment advice?

Exercise 2-9 Accounting rate of return method – Replacement decision

Compute the accounting rate of return for the investment in exercise 2–7. We decided there whether it was useful to replace the old production line with the help of the profit comparison method.

a) Using the accounting rate of return method, prepare calculations to show whether the machine should be replaced. The decision criterion used is 13 % for the return on average capital employed.

b) Explain in general if the investment should regarded as worthwhile under the conditions described.

Exercise 2-10 Accounting rate of return method and payback method – Comparison of alternatives

A residence administering agency plans to purchase a new IT system in order to better control receiving rents and to adjust rents to market conditions sooner. Presently the agency has a loss in revenue due to this deficiency. A modern IT system could overcome this deficiency.

The goal of the following investment appraisal is to decide if the purchase of the IT system is profitable. The system can be purchased as well as leased.

The following financial details are known:

- Current annual loss: € 50,000
- Costs for the software: € 152,000, payable at delivery, hence at the beginning of the economic life
- Maintenance: € 1,300 per month
- Interest rate: 6 %
- Economic life: 6 years

a) Calculate the payback of the computer systems.

b) The management is using a four-year maximum payback criterion for investments. What advice would you give?

c) What is the investment project's accounting rate of return? What would your advice be if the minimum acceptable level of the accounting rate of return were 8 %?

Exercise 2-11 Payback method – Replacement decision

For the investment in exercise 2–7 resp. exercise 2–9 we now compare the project by means of the payback method in addition to the already calculated profit comparison and comparison of accounting rates of return. Use a payback acceptance period of 5 years.

a) First evaluate the decision criterion in general.

b) Calculate the non-discounting payback based on average annual cash flow, and recommend the alternative that should be chosen.

Exercise 2-12 Diverse methods of non-discounting investment appraisal

The health resort 'Nice Beach' on an island in the North Sea wants to enhance their service for the two million guests on one hand and to make the billing of the visitor's tax more efficient on the other hand. Therefore, they intend to introduce a so-called guest card with the following functions:

- It serves as a ferry ticket from the mainland to the island.
- It serves as a visitor's card and allows for use of the various offerings of the resort administration.
- It enables certain services like the reservation of a beach chair.

The card has to be designed so that all relevant payments can be made conveniently at a machine upon leaving the island. It is expected that already in the year of introduction, the annual cost of personnel in the resort administration can be reduced by € 120,000.

There is a choice between two systems: The initial capital expenditure for system A is € 1,500,000 and for system B € 2,000,000. We assume that both systems have the same quality. The economic life is assumed to be 10 years in either case. No salvage values occur at the end of the useful life expectancy. The resort administration calculates for investment decisions with an interest rate of 6 %.

2.7 Exercises with Answers

Additional costs occur as follows:

	System A	System B
Material price of the guest card per guest	€ 0.05	€ 0.02
Annual energy costs	€ 500	€ 400
Annual maintenance	€ 5,000	included in the initial outlay

a) Assess the alternatives using the cost comparison method. Imputed interest is based on the average capital employed.

b) Using the profit comparison method, what would your decision advice be? Would your advice differ from part a?

c) Expand your calculation by taking into account the size of the initial investment. Perform an accounting rate of return comparison.

d) Finally, complete your reflections by applying the non-discounting payback method.

e) Which system would you advise to accept?

2.7.2 Answers

Answer to exercise 2-1 Cost comparison method – Comparison of alternatives

	Brand A	Brand B
Depreciation	3,000	2,500
Imputed interest	1,200	1,000
Fixed costs	1,500	1,200
Operating expenses	12,000	14,400
Total costs	17,700	19,100
Costs per punching act	0.44	0.42

Although the total costs of brand B are higher, it is nevertheless more favourable because the costs per punching act are lower. In this case the unit costs must be compared.

Answer to exercise 2-2 Cost comparison method – Comparison of alternatives with salvage values

a)

	Copy machine A	Copy machine B
Depreciation	2,000	4,000
Imputed interest	375	750
Maintenance	2,000	500
Operating expenses	500	300
Total costs	4,875	5,550

Copy machine A represents the better investment due to the lower average annual costs.

b)

	Copy machine A	Copy machine B
Depreciation	1,900.00	3,000.00
Imputed interest	393.75	937.50
Maintenance	2,000.00	500.00
Operating Expenses	500.00	300.00
Total costs	4,793.75	4,737.50

The higher salvage value of copy machine B reverses the preference. Now, copy machine B is better.

Answer to exercise 2-3 Cost comparison method – Comparison of alternatives with critical values

First the annual fixed costs are calculated. Then the critical activity quantity is computed.

	Alternative I	Alternative II
Depreciation	100,000	125,000
Imputed interest	20,000	25,000
Other costs	60,000	70,000
Personnel costs	210,000	240,000
Total fixed costs	390,000	460,000

2.7 Exercises with Answers

Calculation of the critical quantity:

€ 390,000 + x × € 150 = € 460,000 + x × € 130

$\Leftrightarrow$ x × € 20 = € 70,000

$\Leftrightarrow$ x = 3,500

If the quantity exceeds 3,500 units, then alternative II is preferable.

We check by substituting in this value of 3,500 units to confirm that the total costs are then equal for both alternatives. As can be seen from the following table this condition is fulfilled.

	Alternative I	Alternative II
Depreciation	100,000	125,000
Imputed interest	20,000	25,000
Other costs	60,000	70,000
Personnel costs	210,000	240,000
Total fixed costs	390,000	460,000
Variable costs	525,000	455,000
Total costs	915,000	915,000

Answer to exercise 2-4 Cost comparison method – Replacement decision

	Old	New
Depreciation	-	6,000
Imputed interest	-	1,200
Maintenance	15,000	1,000
Total costs	15,000	8,200
Advantage for the new car		6,800

Because of the remaining fixed costs for the old car the calculation can be simplified by ignoring depreciation and imputed interest for the old vehicle. Other fixed costs and operating expenses need no consideration because they are equal in both alternatives.

Answer to exercise 2-5 Profit comparison method – Comparison of alternatives

First the annual depreciation is calculated:

€ 144,000 ÷ 6 years = € 24,000/year

The imputed interest is $\dfrac{€144,000}{2} \times 0.06 = €\,4,320$.

The annual average profit is calculated as follows:

Revenues (saved personnel costs)	€ 65,000
– Depreciation	€ 24,000
– Imputed interest	€ 4,320
– Costs from lower usability	€ 20,000
– Maintenance	€ 3,680
= Profit	€ 13,000

If the capital could be invested into another investment generating a profit of € 14,000, the investment in the harvesting machine would not be preferable.

Answer to exercise 2-6 Profit comparison method – Comparison of alternatives with critical values

a)

	Model A	Model B
Depreciation	85,000	100,000
Imputed interest	21,250	25,000
Other fixed costs per year	20,000	20,000
Variable Costs per year	70,000	63,000
Annual revenues	336,000	350,000
Average annual profit	139,750	142,000

Model B has the higher average annual profit and is, therefore, preferred using this method.

2.7 Exercises with Answers

b)

First we derive the profit functions for both alternatives:

$P_A = x \times (€ 4.8 - € 1) - € 126{,}250 = x \times € 3.8 - € 126{,}250$

$P_B = x \times (€ 5 - € 0.9) - € 145{,}000 = x \times € 4.1 - € 145{,}000$

Equating these functions yields:

$x \times € 3.8 - € 126{,}250 = x \times € 4.1 - € 145{,}000$

$\Leftrightarrow \quad € 18{,}750 = x \times € 0.3$

$\Leftrightarrow \quad x = 62{,}500$

If the amount of users exceeds 62,500, then the more expensive model B is preferable.

c)

A check can be made by substituting in these values:

	Model A	Model B
Depreciation	85,000	100,000
Imputed interest	21,250	25,000
Other annual fixed costs	20,000	20,000
Variable costs per year	62,500	56,250
Annual revenues	300,000	312,500
Annual average profit	111,250	111,250

The check shows that the result in subtask b is correct. The average annual profit is equal in both cases.

Answer to exercise 2-7 Profit comparison method – Replacement decision

	Old production line	New production line
Depreciation	-	3,000,000
Imputed interest	-	1,950,000
Maintenance	5,000,000	500,000
Variable costs	40,000,000	42,900,000
Revenues	60,000,000	66,000,000
Average annual profit	15,000,000	17,650,000

Because of the remaining fixed costs for the old production line, the calculation can be simplified by ignoring depreciation and imputed interest for the old production line. We observe that the replacement would generate a higher annual profit by € 2,650,000. Accordingly, the replacement is worthwhile.

Answer to exercise 2-8 Accounting rate of return method – Comparison of alternatives

$$\text{Accounting rate of return} = \frac{\text{Average annual profit}}{\text{Average capital employed}} \times 100$$

With an anticipated economic life of 10 years, we get the following annual depreciation rates: € 15,000 ÷ 10 years = € 1,500. The revenues are calculated as follows: € 2.00 × 150 hours × 12 months = € 3,600. Note: Only the difference between the old and the new rental fee is regarded, because it is directly influenced by the investment.

Imputed interest is not regarded because we want to calculate the investment's rate of return. If that interest were taken into account, only the rate of return exceeding it would be calculated.

The average annual profit is calculated as follows:

Revenues	€ 3,600
– Maintenance agent	€ 175
– Depreciation	€ 1,500
= Profit	€ 1,925

$$\text{Average annual capital employed} = \frac{\text{Initial outlay}}{2} = \frac{€\,15{,}000}{2} = €\,7{,}500$$

So the accounting rate of return is

$$\frac{€\,1{,}925}{€\,7{,}500} \times 100 = 25.6\,\%$$

Since the accounting rate of return is clearly above the required rate of 4 %, the investment is acceptable.

Answer to exercise 2-9 Accounting rate of return method – Replacement decision

a)

We calculated that the replacement would generate a higher annual profit of € 2,650,000. However, this value cannot simply be transferred into the accounting rate of return method,

2.7 Exercises with Answers

because it contains imputed interest which remains unconsidered with the accounting rate of return method. Therefore, this calculation must be corrected by the imputed interest. We get:

	Old production line	New production line
Depreciation	-	3,000,000
~~Imputed interest~~	-	~~1,950,000~~
Maintenance	5,000,000	500,000
Variable costs	40,000,000	42,900,000
Revenues	60,000,000	66,000,000
Average annual profit	15,000,000	19,600,000

	New production line
Difference in annual profit	4,600,000
Average capital employed	15,000,000
Accounting rate of return in %	30.7

b)

Within the framework of the replacement comparison, those investment projects are worthwhile whose lower costs respective to higher profits guarantee a certain rate of return of the employed capital. The result can be directly compared to the company's target accounting return on investment. In this case the replacement would be acceptable.

Answer to exercise 2-10 Accounting rate of return method and payback method – Comparison of alternatives

a)

$$\text{Payback period} = \frac{\text{Inital outlay}}{\text{average annual cash flow}}$$

$$\frac{€\,152,000}{€\,50,000 - €\,15,600} = \frac{€\,152,000}{€\,34,400} = 4.4 \text{ years}$$

The average annual cash flow is calculated by subtracting the maintenance cost from the revenues. Depreciation and imputed interest are ignored.

b)

As a result the investment is not worthwhile with regard to the criterion length of payback. But we should remember that the payback method is only an additional means of investment appraisal. To make a final decision on the investment we should calculate the accounting rate of return.

c)

$$\text{Accounting rate of return} = \frac{\text{Average annual profit}}{\text{Average capital employed}} \times 100$$

With an anticipated economic life of 6 years, we get the following annual depreciation rates: € 152,000 ÷ 6 years = € 25,333.

The annual variable costs are the costs for maintenance at the amount of € 1,300 per month (= € 15,600 per year).

The average annual profit is calculated as follows:

Revenues (current loss in revenues):	€ 50,000
– Depreciation	€ 25,333
– Variable costs	€ 15,600
= Profit	€ 9,067

$$\text{Average annual capital employed} = \frac{\text{Initial outlay}}{2} = \frac{€152,000}{2} = €76,000$$

So the accounting rate of return is

$$\frac{€9,067}{€76,000} \times 100 = 11.9\%.$$

This value is to be compared to the required minimum rate of return and then the desirability of the investment has to be judged. In this case the investment is acceptable since 11.9 % is above 8 % which was the company's target average accounting rate of return.

Answer to exercise 2-11 Payback method – Replacement decision

a)

The replacement decision can be made by means of the payback method. Then the old asset is abandoned only if it pays back the initial capital outlay through annual cost savings or annual increase in profit within the predetermined maximum acceptable time.

b)

	New asset
Initial outlay	30,000,000
Average annual increase in profit	2,650,000
Depreciation (to be added)	3,000,000
Imputed interest (to be added)	1,950,000
Payback period in years	3.95

2.7 Exercises with Answers

The payback is calculated as follows: The initial outlay of € 30 Mio. is divided by € 7.6 Mio. Depreciation is added to the profit because it was subtracted before to calculate the firm's profit. However, depreciation is not a cash outflow. Money does not flow out. The same argumentation stands in regard to imputed interest which has been calculated in excess of debit interest.

This value has to be compared to the maximum acceptable payback period. The project has a payback of approximately 4 years and so is acceptable according to the decision criterion.

Answer to exercise 2-12 Diverse methods of non-discounting investment appraisal

a)

	System A	System B
Depreciation	150,000	200,000
Imputed interest	45,000	60,000
Material	100,000	40,000
Energy	500	400
Maintenance	5,000	0
Total Cost	300,500	300,400

b)

	System A	System B
Saved personnel costs	120,000	120,000
- Total costs	300,500	300,400
= Annual profit	-180,500	-180,400

Advice:

- Due to the fact that the revenues are the same the profit comparison method ranks both systems equally as does the cost comparison method.
- However, we realise that the investment project should be rejected. The decision advice is to accept only those investment projects with positive profits.

c)

	System A	System B
Profit after interest	-180,500	-180,400
+ imputed interest	45,000	60,000
= Profit before interest	-135,500	-120,400
Average capital employed	750,000	1,000,000
Accounting rate of return in %	-18.07	-12.04

Thus we only compare the two alternatives, but not the complete investment strategies, because we did not take into account the return of the € 500,000 left over by choosing system B at the beginning of the decision. If this value had also been regarded, we could possibly still get a positive accounting rate of return for system A.

d)

	System A	System B
Profit after interest	-180,500	-180,400
+ Depreciation	150,000	200,000
+ Imputed interest	45,000	60,000
= Cash Flow	14,500	79,600
Initial outlay	1,500,000	2,000,000
Payback period in years	103	25

Alternative Approach:

	System A	System B
Initial outlay	1,500,000	2,000,000
Cash inflow	120,000	120,000
- Cash outflow	105,500	40,400
= Cash flow	14,500	79,600
Payback period in years	103	25

e)

All methods point to a preference for system B over system A. However, an investment in neither system would be worthwhile because profit is below zero, the accounting rate of return is negative and the payback period considerably exceeds the economic life of the asset.

3 Discounting Methods of Investment Appraisal

3.1 Learning Objectives

In the previous chapter non-discounting methods of investment appraisal were examined. The intention of this chapter is to provide an overview of the discounting methods of investment appraisal. Upon its completion the reader will be able to

- understand what the main discounting methods of investment appraisal are;
- apply the financial mathematics involved in the discounted cash flow techniques and
- gain an insight into the advantages and disadvantages of each presented method.

Furthermore, the comparison of alternatives and the replacement decision are presented as major problems of investment decisions. Salvage values at the end of the estimated life of the asset no longer require a separate section because by the discounting methods of investment appraisal they are treated like normal cash inflows. Exercises and answers will deepen and consolidate the understanding of the discounting methods of investment appraisal.

3.2 Time Value of Money

3.2.1 Basic Example

To start with, we refer to an easy example. Consider a firm that wants to buy a new car. Table 3-1 describes the alternatives to assess:

Table 3-1 Basic example of the time value of money

	Vehicle A	Vehicle B
Initital outlay in €	10,000	15,000
Anticipated average life in years	5	5
Interest rate in %	5	5
Maintenance and repair in € per year	1,250	125

To identify the differences between the non-discounting and discounting methods of investment appraisal in Table 3-2 we begin again by applying the cost comparison method:

Table 3-2 Cost comparison for the basic example

	Vehicle A	Vehicle B
Depreciation	2,000	3,000
Imputed interest	250	375
Maintenance and repair	1,250	125
Total costs	3,500	3,500

The cost comparison method does not lead to a correct decision, because the average total costs per year are equal. If we additionally assume that both alternatives yield average annual receipts of € 5,000 and afterwards run the profit method, then again both alternatives are ranked the same. The annual average accounting profit is € 1,500 for vehicle A as well as for vehicle B.

Discounting methods take into account the time value of money.[8] An amount of money which has to be paid or is earned 'today' does not have the same value as an amount of money which has to be paid or is earned 'tomorrow'. We need to convert all cash flows paid or received at different points of time to a common reference point. This could be a point at the end of the economic life of the asset. However, it makes the concept more readily understandable to use the present time as reference point. First it allows for an easier comparison of investment projects with different lengths of life. Second it is easier to compare the amount of money to be expended now to buy the asset with the present value of a stream of cash flows.

---

[8] Therefore you won't find depreciation rates in the discounting methods of investment appraisal. The depreciation rate is calculated to generate a firm's profit. It represents nothing but an accounting convention which allows spreading the initial cost of an asset over its estimated economic life. The discounting methods use the actually paid cash outflow for the initial investment instead.

3.2.2 Compounding and Discounting

We look at the capital growth of a certain initial amount of money (here € 1,000) over time. What would be the future value V_1 of the initial value V_0 after one year? In twelve months time there is still the initial amount deposited plus interest on this initial capital. We assume that this interest is reinvested, thus increasing the level of investment in time.

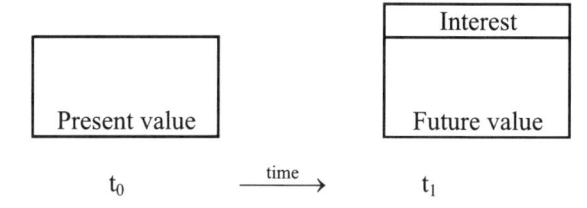

```
    ┌─────────────┐                ┌─────────────┐
    │             │                │   Interest  │
    │             │                ├─────────────┤
    │Present value│                │ Future value│
    └─────────────┘                └─────────────┘
         $t_0$         ──time→          $t_1$
```

We assume 8 % interest, compounded annually.

For V_1 in our example we get:

$V_1 = €\,1{,}000 + €\,1{,}000 \times 0.08$

$V_1 = €\,1{,}000 \times (1 + 0.08)$

$V_1 = €\,1{,}000 \times 1.08$

$V_1 = V_0 \times 1.08 = €\,1{,}080$

By rearranging the equations we realise that the terminal value in one year's time is equal to the initial amount invested multiplied by the future value interest factor 1.08. To examine this procedure more closely we calculate the terminal value in two years.

$V_2 = €\,1{,}080 + €\,1{,}080 \times 0.08$

$V_2 = €\,1{,}080 \times (1 + 0.08)$

$V_2 = €\,1{,}080 \times 1.08$

$V_2 = V_1 \times 1.08$

$V_2 = V_0 \times 1.08 \times 1.08$

$V_2 = V_0 \times 1.08^2$

The terminal value in two years is given by multiplying the initial amount invested by the future value interest factor 1.08^2.

In the same way after year three, we get:

$$V_3 = V_2 + V_2 \times 0.08$$

$$V_3 = V_2 \times (1 + 0.08)$$

$$V_3 = V_2 \times 1.08$$

$$V_3 = V_0 \times 1.08^2 \times 1.08$$

$$V_3 = V_0 \times 1.08^3$$

The exponent (here 3) represents the number of years for which the initial amount is left deposited. This growth pattern can be generalised:

$$V_n = V_0 \times (1+i)^n = V_0 \times q^n \text{ where i is the interest rate and } q^n \text{ is the future value factor.}$$

So, € 5,000 left on deposit at 8 % interest for two years, yields:

$$V_2 = € 5,000 \times 1.08^2$$

$$V_2 = € 5,000 \times 1.1664$$

$$V_2 = € 5,832$$

The factor $(1+i)^n$ can be found by using a financial calculator, a computer spreadsheet program or the tables in the appendix of this book. We can see how the figures in the mathematical tables in the appendix have been derived. 1.1664 is the compound interest factor for two years at an annual rate of interest of 8 %. Along the top of the tables you find different discount rates. Down the left-hand side of the table is the number of years. For arithmetical convenience it is assumed that cash flows occur instantaneously at the end of the time period in question. Financial tables are useful as quick references for common interest rates and common time periods. Note that the tables present approximations to 4 decimal places. If instead you use a calculator, there can be small rounding differences.

Now we turn to another question. Suppose you need € 40,000 in three years to buy a new car. You can earn 7 % on your money. How much do we have to invest 'today'? The present value of a future payment can be found by rearranging the terms in the compound interest formula:

$$V_0 = \frac{V_n}{q^n} = \frac{1}{q^n} \times V_n$$

3.2 Time Value of Money

$1/q^n$ is called the present value factor. Instead of compounding the money forward into the future, we discount it back to the present. The values for the present value factors are also found in the mathematical tables in the appendix.

$$V_0 = \frac{€\,40{,}000}{1.07^3} = \frac{€\,40{,}000}{1.225} = 0.8163 \times €\,40{,}000 = €\,32{,}652$$

If you want to buy a car for € 40,000 in three years where the annual rate of discount is 7 % initially you need € 32,652. Looking for V_0 if the rate of return, the number of periods and the terminal value are given, means solving for the present value of future cash flow. This modus operandi is called discounting.

3.2.3 Future Value and Present Value of an Annuity

So far, the calculations have involved a single sum. If a limited series of equal cash flow occur at different points in time we can use special future value factors and present value factors which are available as short-cuts. These are the so-called annuity future value factors and annuity present value factors.

If the same cash inflow A, is to be received at the end of each year, its terminal value can be calculated by multiplying this cash flow with the annuity future value factor FVA.

$$V_n = A \times FVA$$

where $FVA = \dfrac{q^n - 1}{q - 1}$

We can easily derive this equation. With such an ordinary annuity of which a level cash flow occurs at the end of each period, the first annual payment will have n-1 years to earn interest, the second annual payment will have n-2 years to earn interest etc. According to this the last payment will earn no interest. To find the future value of an annuity V_n the individual future values have to be summed up for the years n–1 plus 1 for the last payment from period n which earns no interest.

$$V_n = A + Aq + Aq^2 + Aq^3 + \ldots + Aq^{n-2} + Aq^{n-1} = \sum_{i=1}^{n} Aq^{i-1}$$

since:

$$\sum_{i=1}^{n} a^{i-1} = \frac{1-a^n}{1-a} \text{ for any } a \neq 1 \text{ we get:}$$

$$V_n = A \times \frac{q^n - 1}{q - 1}$$

If you want to discount a level annual payment to the present time instead you take special present value factors, the so-called annuity present value factor. Annuity present value factors are nothing else but present value factors for a uniform payment occurring each year. They are calculated by summing up the present value factors for the relevant number of years. The values can be taken like those of the future value of an annuity from the mathematical tables at the end of this book.

$$V_0 = A \times PVA$$

with $PVA = \dfrac{q^n - 1}{q^n (q - 1)}$

3.2.4 Annual Equivalent Factor and Sinking Fund Factor

It is possible to spread a present value over an estimated period into constant payments which occur at the end of each period. This calculation is useful if, for example, a single payment of a life insurance should be split up into equal payments receivable. Analogous considerations are known from the credit system if one asks for a credit's repayment by constant annual payments over a certain number of periods. Therefore, we work with the reciprocal of the annuity present value factor. This factor is called the annual equivalent factor.

$$A = V_0 \times \frac{1}{PVA} = V_0 \times \frac{q^n (q - 1)}{q^n - 1}$$

Finally, we can pursue another idea. We can convert a terminal value into a series of annual cash payments. Therefore, we work with the reciprocal of the annuity future value factor. This factor is called sinking fund factor. The mathematical tables in the appendix provide these factors, too.

$$A = V_n \times \frac{1}{FVA} = V_n \times \frac{q - 1}{q^n - 1}$$

3.2 Time Value of Money

Before moving on to look more closely at the net present value model of investment appraisal, we summarise the basics of the discounting methods because they are so important to understand the time value of money.

3.2.5 Summary of Time Value of Money Calculations

We sum up: At the beginning of the time period we possess the original principal. At the end of the period the process of accumulating interest in an investment and reinvesting the interest also leaves us with the terminal value. This process of compounding leads to terminal values. We can also ask for the current value of some future amount. Instead of compounding the money forward, we discount it back to the present. We solve for the present value.

Compounding a level stream of cash flows can be done with annuity future value factors. Discounting a level stream of cash flows can be done with annuity present value factors. If a present value or a terminal value has to be converted into an annually constant amount of cash with consideration of interest, then annual equivalent factors or sinking fund factors are needed. Table 3-3 summarises the most important symbols and essential formulae in investment appraisal. The examples might be helpful to gain a deeper understanding.

Table 3-3 Symbols for the discounting methods of investment appraisal

Symbol	Designates	Explanation and Example
i	Rate of interest	$i = 0.08$ or 8 %
n	Number of periods	e. g. 4 periods, 4 years
$q^n = (1+i)^n$	Future value factor	The future value factor or compound interest factor describes the growth of a beginning value V_0 by compound interest to an ending value V_n. With $n = 4$ years and an interest rate of 8 % the compound interest factor 1.08^4 equals 1.3605. This means: € 100 invested for four years at a 8 % compound interest rate would grow to € 136.05.
$\frac{1}{q^n} = q^{-n}$	Present value factor	The present value factor is the reciprocal of the future value factor. With the help of the present value factor we can calculate the present value of an amount of money which has been deposited over n years. What was the beginning amount invested of € 136.05 to be paid in 4 years, assuming a 8 % interest rate? Answer: $\frac{1}{q^n} = \frac{1}{1.08^4} = 0.7350$. € 136.05 × 0.7350 = € 100.

$\dfrac{q^n - 1}{q - 1}$	Annuity future value factor	With the help of a annuity future value factor we calculate the future value of a level stream of cash flows. A company wants to put away money each year to replace an asset when it wears out. If you deposit € 25,000 at the end of each year for 5 years with the account paying 7 % annual interest, the future value is: € 25,000 × 5.7507 (FVA for 5 years and 7 %) = € 143,768.
$\dfrac{q^n - 1}{q^n(q - 1)}$	Annuity present value factor	The annuity present value factor is calculated by summing up the present value factors. It is used to discount a level income stream. Consider an investment that will pay you € 25,000 at the end of each year for 5 years. You could earn 7 % a year if you invested your money elsewhere. The present value is: € 25,000 × 4.1002 (PVA for 5 years and 7 %) = € 102,505.
$\dfrac{q - 1}{q^n - 1}$	Sinking fund factor	Sinking fund factors are used to convert a terminal value into a series of level annual cash payments allowing for interest. Suppose you want to replace an asset in three years for € 20,000. How much money do you have to save each year when the rate of discount is 6 %? The calculation is: € 20,000 × $\dfrac{1}{FVA}$ (for 3 years and 6 %) = € 20,000 × $\dfrac{1}{2.6730}$ = € 20,000 × 0.3741 = € 7,482.
$\dfrac{q^n(q - 1)}{q^n - 1}$	Annual equivalent factor	Annual equivalent factors are used to convert a present value into a series of level annual cash payments allowing for interest. What amount can we withdraw at the end of each year on an initial investment of € 20,000 at 6 % interest for 3 years? The calculation is: € 20,000 × $\dfrac{1}{PVA}$ (for 3 years and 6 %) = € 20,000 × $\dfrac{1}{3.1836}$ = € 20,000 × 0.3141 = € 6,282.

3.3 Net Present Value Method

3.3.1 Introduction

The net present value method works on the principle that an investment is a worthwhile undertaking if the money got out of the investment exceeds the money put in. However, payments occurring at different points of time cannot be compared directly. They have to be converted to a common reference point, the present time respective to the decision point of time. This makes the concept more readily understandable.

3.3 Net Present Value Method

The net present value is calculated by discounting the investment's cash inflow as well as the investment's cash outflow to the present time which is the time before undertaking the investment. All relevant cash flows are incremental future cash flows. The sunk costs, what is those that have already been incurred prior to the investment are, therefore, not relevant.[9] The project's cash flow is discounted at a specified rate, namely the market rate of interest, cost of capital or the opportunity cost.

Now we calculate the net present value for the following example: Initial outlay € 70,000, economic life 3 years and interest rate 7 %. The cash flow is as illustrated in Table 3-4.

Table 3-4 Investment's payments within the example

	Cash outflow in €	Cash inflow in €
End of year 1	10,000	50,000
End of year 2	10,000	50,000
End of year 3	15,000	40,000

To calculate the net present value we set up Table 3-5. For each year cash inflows and cash outflows are discounted, i.e. multiplied by the respective present value factor and thus converted to the decision point in time.

Table 3-5 Calculation of present values within the example

Year	PVF at 7 %	Cash inflow	Cash outflow	Cash flow	Present value cash flow
1	0.9346	50,000	10,000	40,000	37,384.00
2	0.8734	50,000	10,000	40,000	34,936.00
3	0.8163	40,000	15,000	25,000	20,407.50
Total					92,727.50

As the initial outlays are normally assumed to occur at the beginning of year 1, we finish the calculation as follows:

Present value cash flow	€ 92,727.50
– Present value initial outlay	€ 70,000.00
= Net present value	€ 22,727.50

---

[9] Cash flow estimation is a complex task. For quantitative and qualitative techniques of forecasting cash flows cf. Dayananda, Don, et al., Capital Budgeting: Financial Appraisal of Investment Projects, Cambridge 2002, pp. 37-73.

Figure 3-1 illustrates this analysis in the form of a time line.

Figure 3-1 Time line illustration of a net present value

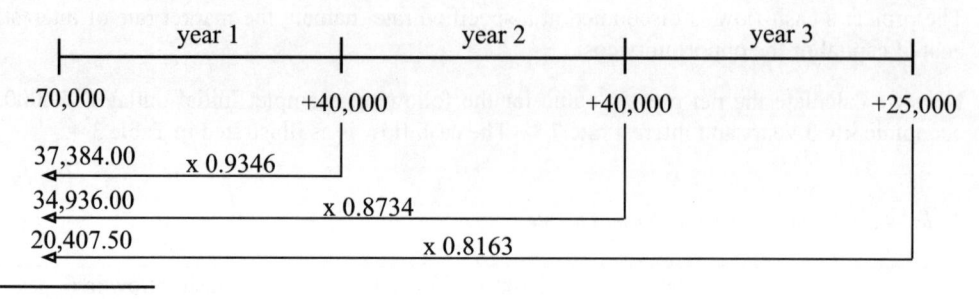

```
                year 1                  year 2                  year 3
       |————————————————|————————————————|————————————————|
   -70,000            +40,000           +40,000          +25,000

   37,384.00    x 0.9346
   34,936.00                x 0.8734
   20,407.50                                 x 0.8163
   ─────────
   22,727.50
```

Usually it is not necessary to discount the initial outlay any further. If it occurs at the beginning of year 1, then it is already a present value. If it occurs later, then the payments for the initial capital outlay must be discounted to their present value. Possibly generated liquidation values are treated like normal cash inflow.

What does a net present value of € 22,727.50 mean?

1. If the investment project is financed with equity, then the capital invested is completely paid back and in addition, the project produces an excess return of € 22,727.50 in comparison to an investment on the capital market.
2. If the initial outlay was borrowed, then the project would generate a sufficient cash flow to pay the interest, repay the loan and leave a surplus of € 22,727.50.

In general terms, the net present value can be expressed as follows:

$$\text{NPV} = -(\text{Initial outlay}) + \frac{\text{Cash flow year 1}}{(1+i)^1} + \frac{\text{Cash flow year 2}}{(1+i)^2} + ... + \frac{\text{Cash flow year n}}{(1+i)^n}$$

Briefly, the net present value is the economic profit created by an investment. It is a convenient method of deciding if the future cash benefit is worth the present cost. We should make it a rule to accept all investment projects with a positive net present value, because wealth is created by undertaking the investment. An investment whose net present value equals zero should not be rejected, because the capital invested is paid back and in addition, generates a return at the discount rate. Investment projects with a negative net present value should, therefore, be rejected.

3.3 Net Present Value Method

> The net present value method decision rule is:
>
> - NPV > 0: Accept the project.
>
> - NPV = 0: Indifferent.
>
> - NPV < 0: Reject the project.
>
> - As far as deciding between mutually exclusive projects is concerned then, an investment 1 is better than an investment 2 if its net present value is greater. This means: $NPV_1 > NPV_2$.

If capital is a limited resource, then management should calculate the so-called profitability index.

$$PI = \frac{NPV}{Initial\ outlay}$$

When available investment funds are limited, the net present value is divided by the initial investment. The profitability index is the value increase per unit money invested. The greater the profitability index, the greater is the relative attractiveness of the investment. Using the profitability index, it is possible to provide a ranking of projects if they are divisible.

Alternatively we can calculate present values if the investment does not deliver any revenue over time. In comparing alternatives which lead only to cash outflows, the alternative with the lower present value of all cash outflows should be chosen.

3.3.2 Role of Financing

To make clear the role of financing for the assessment of an investment project by the net present value method, we refer to the example above again.[10] Instead of discounting the project's cash flow to a present value, the cash flow is compounded forward to a terminal value. The reason for doing so is that this helps to illustrate the reinvestment assumptions. We calculate the terminal value of the investment under the following four assumptions:

1. Investment of € 70,000 on the capital market. This would be the alternative for an investor who has equity at his disposal.
2. Transaction of the investment, financing with equity.
3. Transaction of the investment, financing with debt at 100 % and repayment at the end of the time period in a single sum.
4. Transaction of the investment, financing with debt at 100 % and repayment at the best possible rate.

---

[10] Those who think that these calculations are too complex right now, can first move on to Chapter 3.3.3 and come back later to this point.

The scheme in Table 3-6 is taken from the concept of a complete financial plan.[11] The vital element of the complete financial plan is a table, which shows all payments attributable to an investment project. It is set up so that in columns you find the years of the investment's economic life, in rows the cash inflow and cash outflow of the investment and the financial dispositions.

Along the top of the table in the first row, the economic life of the investment is presented. In row 2 the cash flow of the investment is allocated to the respective years. In each period decisions to achieve a financial equilibrium are taken. Financial requirements lead to a raise of loan, surplus funds are reinvested. Equity (line 3) indicates the opening inventory of ownership capital. Loans are raised at the beginning of the investment as the difference between equity and the initial outlay of the investment and represent a cash inflow for the investor. This explains the positive sign in the first column. Debt leads to the payment of debit interest by the investor, and furthermore he repays the loan according to a declared repayment plan. The negative signs mean that the investor transacts cash outflows.

Deposit generated cash inflows are listed in the rows. Those reinvestments over time depict cash outflows. For this reason they have been given a negative sign. Additional investment is automatically liquidated in the subsequent year. For didactical reasons we assume only one year investments. Those are like the credit interest on these investments flowing to the investor and have a positive sign as a consequence. Credit interest as well as the repayment of money invested is available for disposal in the following period.

The last rows are made for specifying the inventory of debt and deposit. The decision criterion is the investment's terminal value at the end of the economic life which can be taken directly from the complete financial plan. This is the balance of debt and deposit at the end of the relevant planning period.

First we consider in Table 3-6 the case of a pure investment of € 70,000 on the capital market and then as a comparison, in Table 3-7 the transaction of the investment, financed by equity at 100 %.

---

[11] We introduce the concept of the complete financial plan at this stage. We will work with this concept in greater detail in Chapter 5.4. See Grob, Heinz L., Einführung in die Investitionsrechnung, 5th ed., München 2006, pp. 104-126.

3.3 Net Present Value Method

Table 3-6 Complete financial plan, investment of € 70,000 on the capital market

Time period	0	1	2	3
Project cash flow				
Equity	70,000			
Debt				
+ Additional raise of loan				
- Loan repayment				
- Debit interest				
Deposit				
- Additional investment	-70,000	-74,900	-80,143	-85,753
+ Repayment of money invested		70,000	74,900	80,143
+ Credit interest		4,900	5,243	5,610
Inventory				
Debt	0	0	0	0
Deposit	70,000	74,900	80,143	85,753
Balance	70,000	74,900	80,143	85,753

Table 3-7 Complete financial plan, transaction of the investment, financing with equity

Time period	0	1	2	3
Project cash flow	-70,000	40,000	40,000	25,000
Equity	70,000			
Debt				
+ Additional raise of loan				
- Loan repayment				
- Debit interest		0	0	0
Deposit				
- Additional investment		-40,000	-82,800	-113,596
+ Repayment of money invested			40,000	82,800
+ Credit interest			2,800	5,796
Inventory				
Debt		0	0	0	0
Deposit		0	40,000	82,800	113,596
Balance		0	40,000	82,800	113,596

If we made the investment we would generate a terminal value of € 113,596. If one left the equity of € 70,000 on deposit instead, a terminal value of € 85,753 would be generated. Thus the difference between these two values, the terminal wealth gain, is € 27,843. The present value of this terminal wealth gain is € 22,728 if discounted for 3 years at a 7 % annual interest rate. This is exactly the investment's net present value as calculated in Chapter 3.3.1.

Table 3-8 Complete financial plan, Transaction of the investment, financing with debt at 100 % and repayment at the end of the time period in a single sum

Time period	0	1	2	3
Project cash flow	-70,000	40,000	40,000	25,000
Equity				
Debt				
+ Additional raise of loan	70,000			
- Loan repayment				-70,000
- Debit interest		-4,900	-4,900	-4,900
Deposit				
- Additional investment		-35,100	-72,657	-27,843
+ Repayment of money invested			35,100	72,657
+ Credit interest			2,457	5,086
Inventory				
Debt	70,000	70,000	70,000	0
Deposit	0	35,100	72,657	27,843
Balance	-70,000	-34,900	2,657	27,843

Table 3-8 shows as terminal value an amount of € 27,843. We already stated above that this represents a net present value of € 22,728.

Table 3-9 Complete financial plan, Transaction of the investment, financing with debt at 100 % and repayment at the best possible rate

Time period	0	1	2	3
Project cash flow	-70,000	40,000	40,000	25,000
Equity				
Debt				
+ Additional raise of loan	70,000			
- Loan repayment		-35,100	-34,900	0
- Debit interest		-4,900	-2,443	0
Deposit				
- Additional investment			-2,657	-27,843
+ Repayment of money invested			0	2,657
+ Credit interest			0	186
Inventory				
Debt	70,000	34,900	0	0
Deposit	0	0	2,657	27,843
Balance	-70,000	-34,900	2,657	27,843

Even with Table 3-9 the terminal value to be received is € 27,843. We realise that the financing of the investment is irrelevant for the assessment of an investment by the net present value method. The net present value is always € 22,728 regardless how the investment is financed. This makes clear the main assumption of the net present value method. At the discount rate loans can be raised and money can be invested. At this point we do not evaluate

3.3.3 Relevance of Differential Investments

We have learned that two or more investment projects can be compared by calculating their net present values and choosing the investment projects with the highest net present value. Let us now turn to the question of how it is possible to compare investment projects which have differing capital outlays and life-spans with the help of the net present value method. The premise for the validity of this assumption is that differential sums of money can be invested at any scale at the discount rate; because then differential investments have a net present value of zero and need not to be considered explicitly.

To illustrate under what assumptions it makes sense to use the net present value method we compare the already known initial example

Year	0	1	2	3
Cash flow for Investment 1	-70,000	40,000	40,000	25,000

with the following investment project

Year	0	1	2
Cash flow for Investment 2	-65,000	40,000	50,000

We call the first investment 'Investment 1' and the second investment 'Investment 2'. If the investor has € 70,000 to undertake Investment 1 and wants to compare Investment 1 with Investment 2 which needs a capital outlay of only € 65,000, he also has to decide what to do with the € 5,000 left over in case he chooses Investment 2.

Investment alternatives are complete only if the capital outlay and the economic life of the investment are equal. Normally, for alternative investments both the initial outlay and the amount and the period of time of the cash flows will differ. We should remember here that this fact restricts the validity when evaluating the non-discounting methods of investment appraisal.

As can be seen, investment projects 1 and 2 differ in capital outlay and economic life. Furthermore the cash flow in the respective time periods is different. In Tables 3-10 and 3-11 we calculate the net present values for both investments. The discount rate is still 7 %.

---

[12] See Chapters 3 (3.5.3) and 5 (5.4).

Table 3-10 Calculation of the net present value for Investment 1

Point in time	0	1	2	3
Cash flow for Investment 1	-70,000	40,000	40,000	25,000
PVF	1	0.9346	0.8734	0.8163
Discounted value	-70,000	37,383	34,938	20,407
Net present value	22,728			

Table 3-11 Calculation of the net present value for Investment 2

Point in time	0	1	2
Cash flow for Investment 2	-65,000	40,000	50,000
PVF	1	0.9346	0.8734
Discounted value	-65,000	37,383	43,672
Net present value	16,055		

We see that the net present value of Investment 1 exceeds that of Investment 2 by € 6,673. Thus, we would prefer investment 1. In order to illustrate the assumptions of the net present value method, we compare Investment 1 and 2. Therefore, we adjust the payments in Table 3-12 by differential investments. These are payments of the difference between both investments.

Table 3-12 Net present value method and differential investments

Point in time	0	1	2	3
Cash flow for Investment 1	-70,000	40,000	40,000	25,000
Cash flow for Investment 2	-65,000	40,000	50,000	
Differential Investment a	-5,000			6,125
Differential Investment b			-10,000	10,700
Cash flow for Investment 2 new	-70,000	40,000	40,000	16,825
Difference between Inv. 1 and Inv. 2 new				8,175
PVF for 7 %				0.8163
Present value		6,673		

3.3 Net Present Value Method

In Table 3-12 differential Investment 'a' adjusts the payment of the additional € 5,000 for Investment 1 by purchasing a fictitious asset for 3 periods on the capital market. This means compounding the money forward into the future over 3 periods. Differential Investment 'b' adjusts for the different return payment in period 2. The extra investment of € 10,000 is deposited in an interest bearing account for one period. Now we sum up the payments with the two differential investments and get the new Investment 2. It differs from investment 1 only by the different payback of € 8,175 in period 3. Discounting this value by 7 % for 3 years, we get € 6,673. This was exactly the difference between both net present values. Thus we have proved that two or more investments can be compared by the net present value method. This is possible because the net present value of these differential investments is zero. Depositing money and then discounting the terminal value at the discount rate always lead to net present values of zero. The net present value approach automatically takes account of the scale of the initial investment as well as the length of life of the investment opportunities.

In addition, the relative advantage of an investment depends on the discount rate. As the discount rate increases, the net present values of an investment's cash flow gets progressively smaller, passes through zero, and then becomes a negative value. To illustrate this graphically, again we pick up the payments of investment 1 and calculate the net present values for different discount rates. Plotting out the net present values on a graph against the discount rate leads to the net present value profile (Figure 3-2).

Figure 3-2 Net present value profile

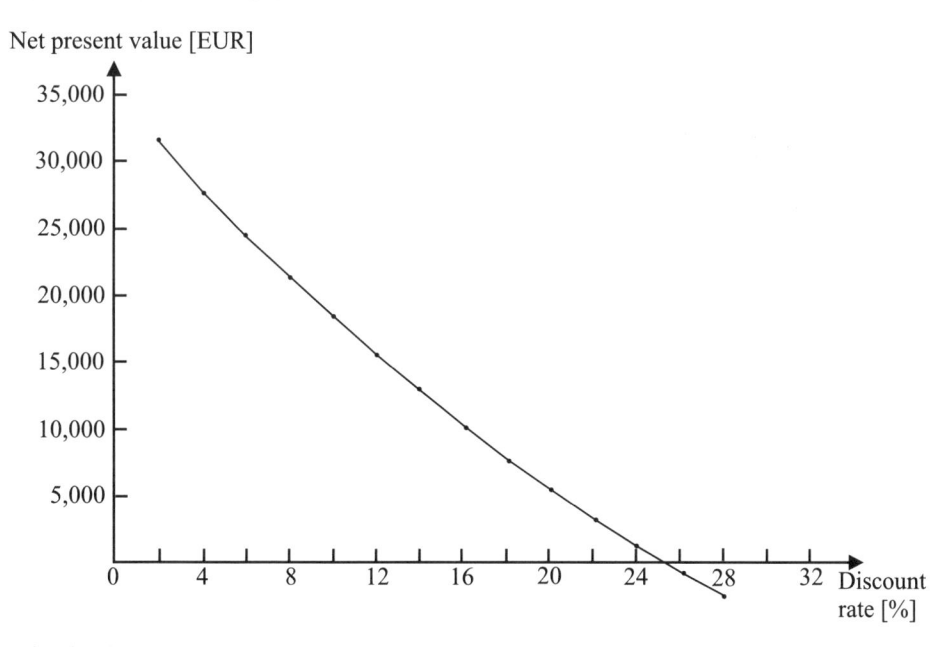

After having examined the basics of the net present value method, we take the opportunity to expand upon our initial problem to decide which vehicle we would advise the car sharing company to buy.

3.3.4 Comparison of Alternatives

In order to compare the alternatives by means of the net present value method, the original data are displayed again for the sake of clarity. According to Table 3-13 we work exactly with the same input data as in the non-discounting methods.

Table 3-13 Basic data for the comparison of alternatives by the net present value method

	AK Rasant	SM Samurai
Initial outlay	9,000	14,000
Economic life in years	2	3
Discount rate in %	5	5
Taxes and insurance	2,000	2,000
Maintenance	1,000	800
Repair	1,500	1,000
Operating expenses	5,250	5,950

Now, we compare the alternatives by means of the net present value method. In contrast to the non-discounting methods we exclude accounting factors such as depreciation or imputed interest. Depreciation is an accounting convention which allows spreading the initial cost of an asset over its estimated economic life. Imputed interest is regarded implicitly over the discount rate. Neither leads to a cash outflow. The other costs do lead to cash outflow at the same amount of money and are, therefore, considered in the net present value method as well. In Table 3-14 these are taxes, insurance, maintenance, repair and operating expenses. We assume that they are paid in one sum at the end of the year.

Table 3-14 Calculation of current cash outflow for the comparison of alternatives by the net present value method

	AK Rasant	SM Samurai
Taxes and insurance	2,000	2,000
Maintenance	1,000	800
Repair	1,500	1,000
Operating expenses	5,250	5,950
Total cash outflow per period	9,750	9,750

The net present value in Table 3-15 is calculated by multiplying the total cash outflow per period by its present annuity value. The initial outlay has to be paid at the beginning of year one and so it is not necessary to discount its value.

3.3 Net Present Value Method

Table 3-15 Calculation of net present values for the comparison of alternatives without cash inflow

	AK Rasant	SM Samurai
Initial outlay	9,000	14,000
PVA	1.8594	2.7232
Total cash outflow per period	9,750	9,750
Net present value	-27,129	-40,551

According to this the AK Rasant would be the preferable vehicle, because the respective discounted cash outflow is lower. However, we have made one mistake. So far we have not taken into account that the cash inflow for the two vehicles differ. The calculation above would be complete if both vehicles generated an equal cash inflow or if they generated no cash inflow at all. Cash inflow is taken into account in the following calculation. The net present value in Table 3-16 is calculated by subtracting the present value of all cash outflows and the initial outlay from the present value of all cash inflows.

Table 3-16 Calculation of net present values for the comparison of alternatives with cash inflows

	AK Rasant	SM Samurai
Initial outlay	9,000	14,000
PVA	1.8594	2.7232
Cash outflow per period	9,750	9,750
Cash inflow per period	17,150	17,850
Net present value	4,760	8,058
Difference between net present values		3,298

The vehicle type SM Samurai has the greater positive net present value at € 3,298 and is, therefore, preferred.

3.3.5 Replacement Decision

There is no difference in the application of the net present value method between asset expansion projects and asset replacement projects. The difference lies in the calculation of the relevant cash flows. This question often has to be addressed in practice: How long should a company spend money maintaining an existing asset, and when should it be replaced by a new one? This is clearly a choice between mutually exclusive investments. At this point I would like to present a limitation of the following analysis. We implicitly assume an unchanging technology and repeat purchases over time which is seldom the case in practice. If e.g. an old asset can be used for 3 more years, but the new asset would last for 15 years, then to simply rank the assets' net present values will not be sufficient, because one investment provides considerably longer service. In these cases we assume that the investments can be repeated until we arrive at a time horizon at which both assets would be reaching the end of their lives simultaneously. Furthermore, we assume that the asset is needed over this time horizon and that identical assets will be available at equivalent prices in the future. These drawbacks should be kept in mind when assessing investments.

To present the particular characteristics of an asset replacement project we return to our car sharing company. The SM Samurai is currently in use. Its annual cash flow is € 8,100. The current market value of this car is assumed to be € 8,000. For simplicity we ignore taxes on the sale of the old car. In addition, we assume that it will last for 2 more years. It could be replaced by the CSA Chevalier which has been presented in Chapter 2.2.5. Its financial figures are reproduced in Table 3-17 for convenience. Should the SM Samurai be sold and replaced now?

Table 3-17 Basic data for the CSA Chevalier

	CSA Chevalier
Initial outlay	10,000
Economic life	4
Taxes and insurance	1,800
Maintenance	800
Repair	500
Running costs per km	0.12
Sales price per km	0.55

A driving performance of 35,000 kilometres per year will lead to an annual cash flow of: 35,000 km × (€ 0.55 – € 0.12) – € 1,800 – € 800 – € 500 = € 11,950. We compare the two alternatives by using marginal cash flows over a 4 year time horizon. This means that if the old car is kept, another used car needs to be bought for € 8,000 at the end of year 2. The increase in cash flows is € 11,950 (Cash flow from the CSA Chevalier) – € 8,100 (Cash flow from the SM Samurai) = € 3,850. The cost of the old asset is the forgone sales price. At a 5 % discount rate the net present value of the marginal investment to buy the CSA Chevalier is positive. To summarise, this calculation is shown in Table 3-18. As a consequence the SM Samurai should be sold immediately.

3.3 Net Present Value Method

Table 3-18 Marginal cash flows of new car purchase

Year	0	1	2	3	4
Purchase CSA Chevalier	-10,000				
Sell SM Samurai	8,000				
Net initial outlay	-2,000				
Avoid purchase of another SM Samurai			8,000		
Incremental cash flow		3,850	3,850	3,850	3,850
Total cash flow	-2,000	3,850	11,850	3,850	3,850
PVF at 5 %	1	0.9524	0.9070	0.8638	0.8227
Present value	-2,000	3,667	10,748	3,326	3,167
Net present value	18,908				

3.3.6 Evaluation of the Net Present Value Method

1. A precondition for applying the net present value method correctly is an accurate forecast of all the relevant project's cash flows.

2. When comparing mutually exclusive investments, choose the one with the maximum net present value, given that the value is positive. If the investment does not generate any cash flow, then choose the one which has a series of costs with the lowest present value.

3. It was demonstrated that the net present value can be adapted to support project ranking in the context where mutually exclusive investment opportunities have unequal lives, size disparities or cash flow pattern disparities.

4. The choice between investment projects is carried out on the basis of an automatic comparison with the capital market.

5. Care should be taken in not being misled by the financing of an investment. The financing does not affect the way the net present value approach is carried out.

6. The net present value method has no serious flaws. It provides definite decision advice for investments.

3.4 Annuity Method

3.4.1 Introduction

The annuity method is not an alternative ranking method but simply a convenient way to develop the net present value for mutually exclusive investments with unequal lives. It might be used in addition to the net present value method. Its theoretical underpinning is exactly that of the net present value method and hence requires the same evaluation. The total net present value is re-expressed as streams of equivalent annual benefits. Thus, an annuity reflects the investment's equal average annual benefit.[13]

> The decision criteria for the annuity method are:
>
> - A single investment is acceptable if its annuity is positive. This means: A > 0.
>
> - In the context of mutually exclusive investments, then an investment 1 is better than an investment 2 if its annuity is larger. This means: $A_1 > A_2$.

We know how to calculate the net present value with annual constant cash flow: Net present value = PVA × annual constant cash flow. This annual constant cash flow is called annuity. It follows that:

$$\text{Net present value} = \text{PVA} \times \text{Annuity}$$

$$\Leftrightarrow \text{Annuity} = \frac{\text{Net present value}}{\text{PVA}}$$

$$\Leftrightarrow \text{Annuity} = \frac{1}{\text{PVA}} \times \text{Net present value}$$

The annuity method gives a ranking the same as that achieved by the net present value if the compared investment projects have equal economic lives or are repeated to a comparable time horizon.

---

[13] Alternatively the annuity of cash inflows could be compared to the annuity of cash outflows. Then a single investment is worthwhile if the annuity of cash inflows exceeds the annuity of cash outflows.

3.4.2 Comparison of Alternatives

In our continuing example, we refer to the comparison of alternatives which we have already made. The calculated net present value for the vehicle type SM Samurai was € 8,058 with a discount rate of 5 % and an estimated life of 3 years. The question is how to transform this net present value into an annuity. For a discount rate of 5 % and a life of 3 years the PVA is 2.7232.

The reciprocal of the annuity present value factor is called annual equivalent factor and is calculated as

$$\text{Annual equivalent factor} = \frac{1}{2.7232} = 0.3672$$

This leads to the following annuity: 0.3672 × € 8,058 = € 2,959

What does this value mean? In this case an investor is able to withdraw over three years, which is the economic life of the investment, € 2,959 at the end of each year or an amount of € 8,058 at the beginning of its economic life. Hence, this is not a simple average (€ 8,058 ÷ 3 = € 2,686), but a value which takes into account the time value of money. We must invest the € 8,058 at the beginning of the first year at 5 % and then we can withdraw € 2,959 at the end of each year over three year's time. To make this clear we recalculate this result in Table 3-19.

Table 3-19 Equivalent annuity as annualised net present value

Time period	0	1	2	3
Net present value	8,058			
Balance at year's end, accumulated		8,461	5,777	2,959
- Annuity		2,959	2,959	2,959
= Balance after withdrawing annuity		5,502	2,818	0

Now we convert both the net present values for our cars in the car sharing company into annuities, as illustrated in Table 3-20.

Table 3-20 Comparison of Alternatives by the annuity method

	AK Rasant	SM Samurai
Net present value	4,760	8,058
PVA	1.8594	2.7232
Annuity	2,560	2,959

This confirms the preferability of the SM Samurai. It has the higher annuity and is therefore more desirable. Granted that either alternative can be repeated which is assumed to be the case here or that the alternatives have equal lives, the ranking from the net present value approach does not change.

3.4.3 Replacement Decision

The question remains whether the company should continue to use the existing car, which is assumed to be the SM Samurai, or if it should be replaced by the CSA Chevalier. Our analysis from Chapter 3.3.5 can be simplified by using the annuity method. First calculate the net present values for both cars. These have to be divided by the respective annuity present value factor to arrive at equivalent annuities. These values can be compared easily. Table 3-21 shows that the replacement is worthwhile.

Table 3-21 Calculation of equivalent annuities for the replacement decision

Year	0	1	2	3	4
Using old car	-8,000				
Cash flow		8,100	8,100		
Present value	-8,000	7,714	7,347		
Net present value	7,061				
PVA	1.8594				
Annuity	3,798				
Using new car	-10,000				
Cash flow		11,950	11,950	11,950	11,950
Present value	-10,000	11,381	10,839	10,323	9,831
Net present value	32,374				
PVA	3.5460				
Annuity	9,130				
Difference between the annuities	5,332				

3.4.4 Evaluation of the Annuity Method

1. An annuity represents the level stream of cash flows that have a net present value equal to the one of the initial investment. The total increase in wealth through the investment which occurs in the decision point t_0 is spread evenly over the relevant time horizon.

2. Due to the fact that the annuity is based on the net present value, the annuity method deserves the same evaluation as the net present value method.

3. The equivalent annuity or the annualised net present value is a useful tool to account for uneven lives.

4. An annual value may allow for an easier visualisation of the benefits from an investment than the net present value.

5. Annual values can be more easily considered within capital budgeting than a single value like the net present value.

3.5 Internal Rate of Return Method

3.5.1 Introduction

Using the non-discounting methods of investment appraisal we have already calculated a rate of return of the capital involved in the investment. This can be done equally for the discounting methods of investment appraisal. The internal rate of return is the discount rate which sets the net present value of an investment to zero. Thus, the internal rate of return is found by solving for i in the following equation:

$$0 = -(\text{Initial outlay}) + \frac{\text{Cash flow year 1}}{(1+i)^1} + \frac{\text{Cash flow year 2}}{(1+i)^2} + \ldots + \frac{\text{Cash flow year n}}{(1+i)^n}$$

The internal rate of return is also called critical discount rate of the investment, because a higher discount rate would lead to a net present value of the investment of below zero. The internal rate of return represents a break even rate of return of the investment opportunity. A single investment is profitable, if its internal rate of return exceeds some predetermined cut-off rate of return IRR_{min}. This hurdle rate is usually the market rate of interest which reflects the opportunity cost of the capital employed. To be selected, an investment project must generate a return at least equal to the return available elsewhere on the capital market.

The internal rate of return decision rule is:

- $IRR > IRR_{min}$: Accept the project.

- $IRR = IRR_{min}$: Indifferent.

- $IRR < IRR_{min}$: Reject the project.

- In the context of mutually exclusive investments, an investment project 1 is advantageous to an investment project 2, if its internal rate of return is higher. This means: $IRR_1 > IRR_2$.

In the following section four options to determine the internal rate of return are presented.

Option 1: Even annual cash flow from the investment

Finding the internal rate of return is easy if cash flows are even over the asset's life. We set up this problem as a present value of an annuity problem and refer to the basic formula for the calculation of the net present value:

Net present value = Present value of cash flow – Present value of initial outlay

We rearrange the terms in this equation, because the net present value should be equal to zero:

0 = Present value of cash flow – Present value of initial outlay

$\Leftrightarrow$ Present value of initial outlay = Present value of cash flow

$\Leftrightarrow$ Present value of initial outlay = PVA × Annuity

$\Leftrightarrow$ PVA = $\dfrac{\text{Present value of initial outlay}}{\text{Annuity}}$

After the calculation of the present value annuity factor we can look for the internal rate of return in the mathematical tables in the appendix. An example may help to illustrate this approach:

- Initial outlay: € 100,000
- Economic life: 5 years
- Constant annual cash flow: € 25,000

Substituting in the known values gives us:

$$\text{PVA} = \dfrac{€100{,}000}{€25{,}000} = 4$$

By turning to the table of the present value of an annuity in the appendix, going to the 5 period row, and then going across 3.9927 is found at the 8 % column. It is the value which is nearest to 4. Hence, the internal rate of return is 8 %.

Option 2: Graphical Approximation

If cash flows are uneven over the asset's life, which is usually the case, finding the internal rate of return is more difficult. Then one of the possibilities allows for estimating the internal rate of return by linear interpolation. The fact that the relationship between the net present value and the discount rate is not linear is the reason why this provides only an approxima-

3.5 Internal Rate of Return Method

tion to the value for the internal rate of return. We select any two discount rates and calculate the project's net present value at each discount rate. Plotting out the net present values on a graph against the discount rate leads to a linear function. Its intersection with the horizontal axis shows the internal rate of return. Note that the narrower the bracketing around the actual internal rate of return is taken, the more accurate the estimate for the internal rate of return is.

Option 3: Arithmetic Approximation

Another possibility is to approach the internal rate of return arithmetically.[14] In order to achieve this we employ the basic form of a linear equation.

$$\frac{x - x_1}{y - y_1} = \frac{x_2 - x_1}{y_2 - y_1}$$

For our problem we find the interest rate i on the horizontal axis, the net present value on the vertical axis. Hence, the equation above becomes:

$$\frac{i - i_1}{NPV - NPV_1} = \frac{i_2 - i_1}{NPV_2 - NPV_1}$$

with NPV = 0 based on the definition for the internal rate of return this equation can be written as

$$\frac{i - i_1}{-NPV_1} = \frac{i_2 - i_1}{NPV_2 - NPV_1}$$

$$\Leftrightarrow i - i_1 = (-NPV_1) \frac{i_2 - i_1}{NPV_2 - NPV_1}$$

$$\Leftrightarrow i = i_1 - NPV_1 \frac{i_2 - i_1}{NPV_2 - NPV_1}$$

This approach is only an approximation because the calculated internal rate of return is more inaccurate the more the used interest rates in this calculation differ from the actual internal rate of return.

---

[14] The approximation for the calculation of a function's zero positions is also called Regula Falsi method or false position method.

Option 4: Excel calculation

Due to the fact that corporate decision makers usually have access to a computer, the internal rate of return can readily be calculated using Excel spreadsheets. This is an advantage because the solutions so far are only approximations and furthermore they are quite tedious to perform.

The internal rate of return can be found with Excel by setting up a spreadsheet to compute the net present value. First the net present value is computed with an arbitrarily chosen discount rate in a cell. After having calculated the net present value go to the 'tools' menu and click on the item 'goal seek'. This will pull up a window with the fields 'set cell', 'to value' and 'by changing cell'. You can use the Goal Seek feature when you know the result of a single formula, but not the input value the formula needs to determine a particular result. In the field 'set cell' enter the reference for the cell containing the formula to calculate the net present value. In the field 'to value' you enter a zero, because this is the result wanted. In the field 'by changing cell' you enter the reference for the cell containing the chosen discount rate. After hitting 'enter' the computer will go through numerous iterations to arrive at the discount rate which sets the net present value to zero.

3.5.2 Comparison of Alternatives

In applying the approaches described in our car sharing company compute the net present value with two arbitrarily chosen discount rates (Table 3-22). Graphical and arithmetic approximation based on this data can be used to estimate the internal rate of return for both projects.

Table 3-22 Basic data for graphical and arithmetic approximation of the internal rate of return

	AK Rasant	SM Samurai
Discount rate 5 %	€ 4,760	€ 8,058
Discount rate 10 %	€ 3,843	€ 6,144

An approximation can be found through linear interpolation. The resulting internal rate of return is only estimated because the net present value profile is approximated by a straight line. Figure 3-3 shows the linear interpolation method.

3.5 Internal Rate of Return Method

Figure 3-3 Graphical estimate of the internal rate of return

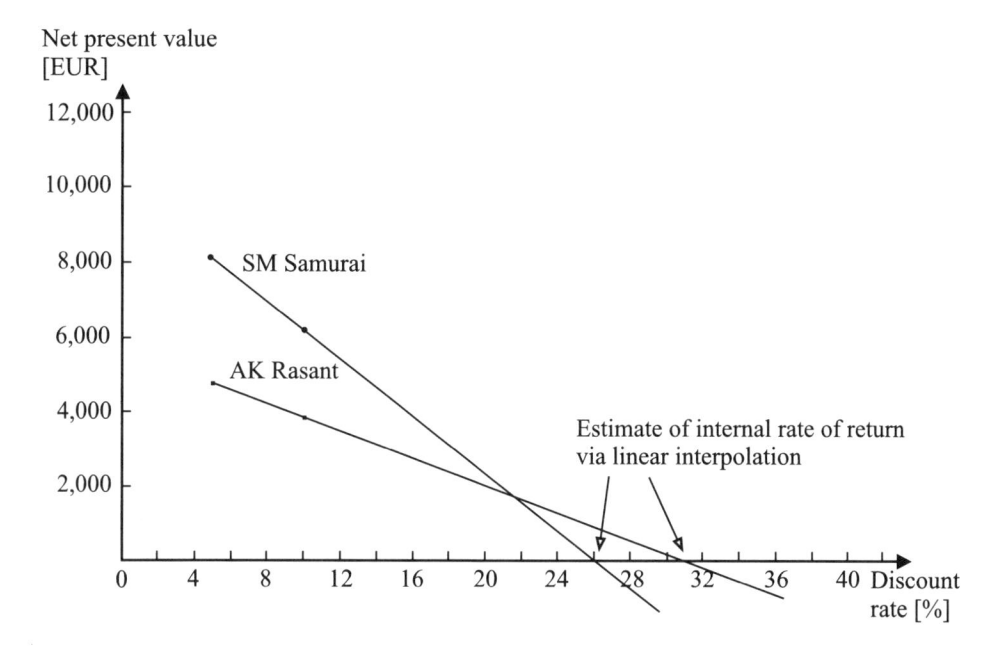

Net present value [EUR]

(graph showing SM Samurai and AK Rasant curves, with "Estimate of internal rate of return via linear interpolation" annotation, x-axis: Discount rate [%] from 0 to 40)

Alternatively we find the internal rate of return by arithmetical approximation.

For the AK Rasant we get:

$$i = 0.05 - €\,4{,}760 \;\frac{0.1 - 0.05}{€\,3{,}843 - €\,4{,}760}$$

$$i = 0.05 - €\,4{,}760 \;\frac{0.05}{€ - 917}$$

$$i = 0.05 + \frac{238}{917}$$

$$i = 0.31 \text{ (rounded)}$$

For the SM Samurai we get:

$$i = 0.05 - €\,8{,}058 \cdot \frac{0.1 - 0.05}{€\,6{,}144 - €\,8{,}058}$$

$$i = 0.05 - €\,8{,}058 \cdot \frac{0.05}{€ - 1{,}914}$$

$$i = 0.05 + \frac{402.9}{1{,}914}$$

$i = 0.26$ (rounded)

Hence, we get an internal rate of return of 31 % for the AK Rasant and an internal rate of return of 26 % for the SM Samurai.

Based on an Excel spreadsheet we obtain the following internal rates of return. (Table 3-23).

Table 3-23 Calculation of internal rates of return by Excel

Discount rate AK Rasant	Present value year 1	Present value year 2		Initial outlay	Net present value
1.41	5,260.5	3,739.5		−9,000	0
Discount rate SM Samurai	Present value year 1	Present value year 2	Present value year 3	Initial outlay	Net present value
1.34	6,063.4	4,538.9	3,397.7	−14,000	0

This illustrates that these values differ significantly from the calculation above. In practice, therefore, the method based on Excel should be preferred. Accordingly the AK Rasant should be preferred because its internal rate of return (41 %) exceeds that of the SM Samurai (34 %).

3.5.3 Internal Rate of Return versus Net Present Value

We compare the results of the internal rate of return method and the net present value method, as shown in Table 3-24:

3.5 Internal Rate of Return Method

Table 3-24 Illustration of investment desirability ranking conflicts

	AK Rasant	SM Samurai
Net present value for i = 5 %	€ 4,760	€ 8,058
Net present value for i = 10 %	€ 3,843	€ 6,144
Internal rate of return	41 %	34 %

We summarise the results from the internal rate of return method and the net present value method: If we use the net present value method, then the SM Samurai would be chosen. If we use the internal rate of return decision rule, then the AK Rasant would be chosen because of the higher internal rate of return. We have to find out which method leads to better investment advice.

If the projects have differing capital outlays and life-spans, then conflicts can occur between the advice given by the net present value decision rule and the advice given by the internal rate of return decision rule. In order to clarify this problem, we graph the net present value profiles of the AK Rasant and the SM Samurai in Figure 3-4. It highlights the ranking conflict between the net present value and the internal rate of return.

Figure 3-4 Net present value profiles for the AK Rasant and the SM Samurai

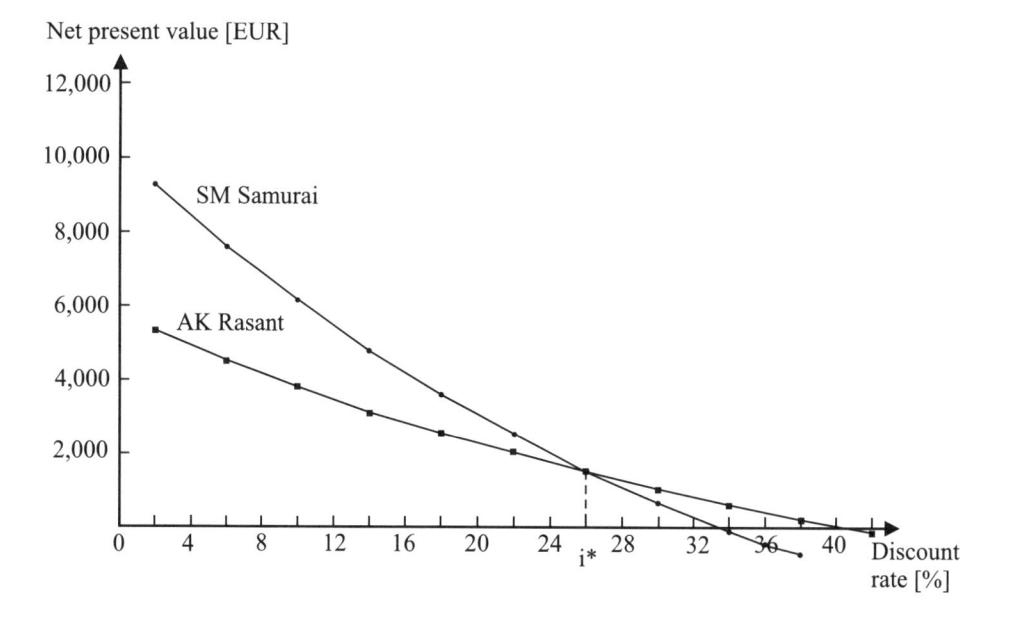

The net present value schedules intersect at one point. On the basis of Figure 3-4 you can see that net present value and internal rate of return lead to identical rankings only if the discount rate exceeds the crossover rate i*. If the discount rate happens to be lower than i*, then the rankings of the two approaches with regard to the investment's profitability are different. We summarise the results in the following overview:

Evaluation according to the net present value method:
- i < i*: The SM Samurai is superior to the AK Rasant.
- i > i*: The AK Rasant is superior to the SM Samurai.

Evaluation according to the internal rate of return method: The AK Rasant is superior to the SM Samurai.

As the internal rate of return and the net present value can give different measures of relative desirability we check the reinvestment assumptions for project-generated cash flows. The net present value method assumes that cash flows are reinvested to earn a rate of return equal to the discount rate. The internal rate of return method implicitly assumes that cash flows are reinvested to earn a rate of return equal to the internal rate of return of the respective project. To find which model is superior we have to clarify which one makes the correct assumption about the reinvestment of a project's cash inflow.

We should realise that there is a logical inconsistency in the internal rate of return's reinvestment assumption, because cash flows generated at the same point in time can be reinvested at a general required rate of return, more so than at the unique internal rate of return. There are no different reinvestment possibilities for different investment opportunities. The rate of return on a particular project relates to that project only. If cash flows at any amount could be reinvested at the internal rate of return rate, then this would represent the general market rate of interest and the discount rate would be equal to the internal rate of return. A modified internal rate of return has been developed to overcome this problem, but this demands very extensive calculations.[15]

Therefore, we conclude: If the net present value method and the internal rate of return method lead to different rankings, then the net present value is superior to the internal rate of return. Accordingly, it is not necessary to make a decision of replacement with the help of the internal rate of return approach.

---

[15] Cf. Lumby, Steve, and Chris Jones, Corporate Finance: Theory and Practice, 7th ed., London 2003, pp. 99-103.

3.5.4 Evaluation of the Internal Rate of Return Method

1. The internal rate of return is the discount rate that makes the estimated net present value of an investment equal to zero. The decision rule is to accept a project if its internal rate of return exceeds the predetermined required return.

2. The internal rate of return method is easy and understandable whereas the net present value is difficult to approach and to communicate and its method of evaluating investment projects is through the use of a user-friendly percentage rate of return which management is familiar with.

3. The implied assumption that any amount of money can be reinvested at the project's internal rate of return is problematic. This assumption is unrealistic and thus less reasonable than the implied assumption of the net present value method that money can be borrowed and reinvested at the discount rate.

4. If the internal rate of return and the net present value give different measures of relative desirability, the net present value approach is superior. The net present value will give correct results if used properly.

3.6 Discounting Payback Method

3.6.1 Introduction

Using the discounting payback method we calculate how long the investment project will take to give returns, but we also allow for the time value of money. We apply the payback method to present value cash flows and not to ordinary cash flows. As with the non-discounting methods an acceptable payback period is chosen, and the company proceeds with projects that meet the acceptable payback criterion.

3.6.2 Comparison of Alternatives

To start with, we calculate the exact payback period for the AK Rasant in table 3-25:

Table 3-25 Calculation of the discounted cumulative cash flow of the AK Rasant

Time	0	1	2
Initial outlay	9,000		
Current value of cash flow		7,400	7,400
PVF		0.9524	0.9070
Present value of cash flow		7,048	6,712
Cumulative present value of cash flow		7,048	13,760

As the cumulative cash flow row shows, all of the cash flow from year 1 and part of the cash flow from year 2 are required to recover the initial investment of € 9,000. In the second year € 9,000 – € 7,048 is needed to reach € 9,000. Since total cash flow for the second year is € 6,712, only a percentage (0.29) of this is needed. Hence, the payback period is:

$$\text{Payback period} = 1 + \frac{€\,9{,}000 - €\,7{,}048}{€\,6{,}712} = 1.29 \text{ years}$$

In Table 3-26 we calculate the exact payback period for the SM Samurai:

Table 3-26 Calculation of the discounted cumulative cash flow of the SM Samurai

Time	0	1	2	3
Initial outlay	14,000			
Current value of cash flow		8,100	8,100	8,100
PVF		0.9524	0.9070	0.8638
Present value of cash flow		7,714	7,347	6,997
Cumulative present value of cash flow		7,714	15,061	22,058

The cumulative cash flow row shows that all of the cash flow from year 1 and part of the cash flow from year 2 are required to recover the initial investment of € 14,000. In the second year € 14,000 – € 7,714 is needed to reach € 14,000. Since total cash flow for the second year is € 7,347, only a percentage (0.86) of this is needed. Hence, the payback period is:

$$\text{Payback period} = 1 + \frac{€\,14{,}000 - €\,7{,}714}{€\,7{,}347} = 1.86 \text{ years}$$

Table 3-27 compares these values to those from the non-discounting payback method:

Table 3-27 Results from non-discounting and discounting payback method

	AK Rasant	SM Samurai
Non-discounting payback period	1.2 years	1.7 years
Discounting payback period	1.3 years	1.9 years

Discounting extends the length of the payback period in comparison to the non-discounting payback, because the cash flow of later periods is weighted lower.

3.6.3 Replacement Decision

Using the non-discounting payback method we compared the incremental capital employed to the annual cost savings or the incremental profit from the investment. To reach this aim we added the depreciation and imputed interest exceeding debit interest of the new investment because they do not represent cash outflow. Using a discounting method, we do not consider average annual savings but savings for each relevant year that is discounted separately.

3.6.4 Evaluation of the Discounting Payback Method

1. The applicability of the discounting payback method is similar to that of the non-discounting payback method. It is still an additional method to assess the risk of an investment. The advantage in comparison to the non-discounting payback method is the better consideration of risk through the concept of discounting because uncertainty grows larger the farther the distance to the decision point is.

2. Furthermore, the discounting payback methods allows for taking into account inflation by using an appropriate discount rate.

3.7 Summary and Evaluation of the Discounting Methods

This chapter has covered the main characteristics of the discounting methods of investment appraisal. They account for the time value of money, and they evaluate projects on the basis of cash flow instead of profit. These were major criticisms of the non-discounting methods, which can be overcome by applying discounting techniques. Accounting profit is a concept developed for reporting the outcome of decisions and not for supporting the actual decision itself. It follows that investment decisions should be based on cash flow. Discounting methods of investment appraisal consider the investment's cash flow and the time at which it is realised. Cash flow arising at different points in time is converted to a common reference point. In general, this is the present time t_0. The net present value approach should be preferred to the internal rate of return because of its reinvestment assumption. Despite the superiority of the net present value approach other criteria are not completely irrelevant and useless. They may be used as supplementary measures to facilitate decision-making.

The following were the main points covered:

1. A pre-condition for a useful application of discounting investment appraisal techniques is the possibility to identify all relevant cash flows.
2. Problems arise if interdependencies with the company's environment exist, e.g. if it is not possible to isolate the outcomes of the investment.
3. So far, we have not considered qualitative investment assessment criteria.
4. Up to this point all techniques presented are based on certain estimates about the input data.
5. In the following chapters we introduce uncertainty as well as qualitative investment assessment criteria. Furthermore we integrate the effects of taxation, inflation and financing the investment if the borrowing and the lending interest rates are not equal. The simplifying assumptions under which the discounting methods of investment appraisal were introduced are put aside step by step.

3.8 Exercises with Answers

3.8.1 Exercises

Exercise 3-1 Basics of the discounting methods of investment appraisal

a) At the beginning of year 1 you can invest € 5,000. If the interest rate is 8 % per annum, how much will you get at the end of year 6?

b) Suppose in three years you would need the sum of € 250,000 to buy land. The bank lends the money at an interest rate of 7 %. How much do you have to invest today?

c) What is the better alternative if the interest rate is 5 %: Getting € 2,000 at the beginning of year 1 or getting € 3,000 at the end of year 4?

d) You could receive € 1,000, then € 2,000 and finally € 3,000 at the end of each of the following 3 years as preliminary payments on your inheritance from your grandfather. You as well as your grandfather could reinvest these payments on the capital market at 8 %. What amount would your grandfather offer alternatively now?

e) What constant amount of money could you withdraw from your bank account over three years at the end of each year if an initial capital of € 20,000 had been invested at 6 %?

3.8 Exercises with Answers

Exercise 3-2 Net present value method I

It is your task to assess two mutually exclusive investment projects:

	Alternative A	Alternative B
Initial outlay	10,000	15,000
Economic life	6	6
Discount rate in %	5	5
Annual cash outflow	1,000	800
Annual cash inflow	3,100	3,900

a) Which alternative would you select for acceptance under the conditions of the net present value method? Explain why.

b) Calculate the net present value for each project, and formulate your investment decision advice. All payments with the exception of the initial outlay are assumed to occur on the last day of the year.

Exercise 3-3 Net present value method II

Through the conversion of a storage building which is currently unused into a flat let for rent, income could be generated. The costs for conversion, occurring at the decision point of time, would be € 35,000. In the following 10 years annual rental income of € 3,500 could be generated, occurring at the end of each year. The discount rate is selected as 4.5 %.

Would you advise to do the reconstruction? Assess the investment with the help of the net present value method.

Exercise 3-4 Net present value method III

Suppose that an investor plans to buy land. Three plots of land could be acquired. They are characterised by the following financial details:

	Land I	Land II	Land III
Initial outlay	€ 45,000	€ 50,000	€ 95,000
Sales value after year 10	€ 80,000	€ 60,000	€ 175,000

State the reason for your evaluation of the purchase using the net present value method (discount rate 4 %). What is your investment decision advice?

Exercise 3-5 Net present value method IV

A company is considering buying new hardware and software. The manufacturer submits three different offers.

1. Immediate purchase of the equipment for € 10,200.
2. Closure of a leasing contract with leasing payments of € 2,400 at the beginning of each year.
3. Closure of a leasing contract with leasing payments of € 2,500 at the beginning of each year over 2 years, and at the beginning of year 3 purchase of the equipment leased so far at € 5,200.

For your calculations assume an economic life of 5 years. The appropriate discount rate is 4 %.

a) Rank the different offers by their net present value.

b) How might the investment decision change if the discount rate increased from 4 % to 10 %?

c) What would your revised investment decision advice be with regard to your calculations in question a if you could negotiate a deferral of payment so that the initial outlay from offer 1 has to be paid at the end of the economic life?

Exercise 3-6 Net present value method V

A landlord considers installing photovoltaic equipment on his roof. Photovoltaic equipment serves solar power generation. It enables the direct transfer of sunlight into electric power. The roof accepts an equipment of 2 kilowatt with maximum sunlight. In Germany, on average 850 kilowatt hours of power can be generated per kilowatt yearly. The original cost of the 2-kilowatt-equipment is € 11,200. The annual operating cost is € 100. The period of use is assumed to be 10 years.

According to the federal law of renewable energy (Erneuerbare-Energie-Gesetz, EEG) the generated energy can be sold to the local utility for a guaranteed price fixed by the government. Thus, the household acts as a power generator subsidised by the government. The guaranteed price is 50 cents per kilowatt hour on average.

Consider for your calculations that all payments occur at the end of each period. Only the initial outlay is due at the beginning of the economic life. Assume that the whole amount of power produced is sold to the local utility. The landlord calculates with an interest rate of 8 %.

3.8 Exercises with Answers

a) Calculate the net present value of the investment.

b) The federal government is subsidising environmental protection energies. The landlord has the opportunity to take out a loan for the initial outlay without paying interest from a publicly owned bank (Kreditanstalt für Wiederaufbau). After two years without repayment he must repay the loan over the next eight years at constant rates. What is the net present value under these conditions?

c) Due to a change in the law, the guaranteed price is set back to 35 cents per kilowatt hour from the fifth year of use on. How does this affect the investment's net present value? Assume the same conditions as in subtask b except for the lower guaranteed price.

d) The landlord makes a last consideration: He assumes an economic life of 20 years, but no lowering of the guaranteed price. Instead he plans assuming a guaranteed price of 50 cents per kilowatt hour over the entire economic life. Recalculate the net present value. Again, except for the changed economic life, assume the same conditions as in subtask b.

e) Justify your results: Under which assumptions would you advise the landlord to accept the investment of solar generated power?

Exercise 3-7 Cost comparison method and net present value method

A company has the opportunity to buy a new van for the car pool. It can choose among three models which are equal in quality. The appropriate discount rate is 4 %. The following data should be used to make a decision:

	Model 1	Model 2	Model 3
Price	€ 72,000	€ 84,000	€ 96,000
Economic life	6 years	6 years	6 years
Annual mileage in kilometres	40,000	40,000	40,000
Operating costs per 100 kilometres	€ 30	€ 25	€ 20
Fixed costs per year	€ 5,200	€ 5,000	€ 4,800

a) Which vehicle would you buy if the decision is based on the cost comparison method?

b) State which investment is worthwhile when using the net present value method? We assume that the current cash outflow occurs at the end of the year, the initial outlay occurs at the beginning of year 1, at the decision point of time.

Exercise 3-8 Annuity method

Refer to the information in exercise 3–4. In that exercise you decided whether the purchase of land was worthwhile. Transfer the net present values into annuities.

Exercise 3-9 Internal rate of return method

An investment can be characterised as follows: Initial outlay: € 60,000 (to be paid at the decision point of time), economic life: 5 years. The estimated cash outflow and cash inflow are as shown in the table:

	Cash outflow in €	Cash inflow in €
End of year 1	20,000	20,000
End of year 2	30,000	30,000
End of year 3	30,000	50,000
End of year 4	35,000	50,000
End of year 5	20,000	60,000

a) Calculate the internal rate of return with the help of the known approximate solution. Use as discount rates i_1 4 % and i_2 6 %.

b) Estimate the internal rate of return using discount rates of i_1 4 % and i_2 10 %. What is noteworthy if you compare your results to those of part a?

c) Set up a calculation within an Excel spreadsheet. What is the proposed investment's internal rate of return? Compare your result to the results from part a and part b.

d) Is the investment worthwhile if the minimum rate of return desired is 9 %?

Exercise 3-10 Accounting rate of return method and internal rate of return method

In a zoo, a new fish basin is to be installed. A capital expenditure of € 150,000 is necessary. The period of use is assumed to be 30 years. Due to the increased attraction of the zoo, the number of visitors is going to increase from 400,000 to 406,250 people annually, paying an entrance fee of € 2.00 each. A further assumption refers to the annual operating costs of € 2,500 for the basin, in addition to the imputed costs.

3.8 Exercises with Answers

a) Using a 6 % minimum interest rate, state whether the investment is worthwhile if you use the accounting rate of return method.

b) Calculate the internal rate of return of the investment.

c) Explain why there is a difference between the interest rate calculated in part b from the accounting rate of return. What are the consequences for your investment advice?

Exercise 3-11 Non-discounting and discounting methods of investment appraisal

To generate warm water, a landlord checks if sun collectors on the roof are a worthwhile investment. The initial outlay would be € 4,000. The economic life is estimated to be 20 years. Experience shows that the installation of sun collectors on equivalent buildings with the orientation of the collectors in the same direction yield savings in energy of 180 kilowatt hours (kWh) per month. For one kilowatt hour € 0.15 must be paid to the local utility. Annual maintenance costs for the sun collectors are € 149.63 €. Alternatively money could be left on deposit at 6 %.

a) How much is the accounting rate of return of the investment? Compute the payback period in addition to that. Measure the length of time in which the initial outlay is recouped.

b) What should the investment advice be with regard to your calculations in question a?

c) Rework problem a on the assumption that a government grant of € 2,000 is awarded, assuming that the savings in electricity remain the same.

d) State whether the investment is worthwhile using both the internal rate of return and the net present value (otherwise identical assumptions as in part c). Assume that the initial outlay has to be paid at the beginning of the first year of use. All other payments occur at the end of the year.

e) Comment critically on the difference between the results from the accounting rate of return method and the internal rate of return method.

3.8.2 Answers

Answer to exercise 3-1 Basics of the discounting methods of investment appraisal

a)

The compound interest factor is 1.5869. Thus the Future value is € 5,000 × 1.5869 = € 7,934.50.

b)

The discount rate is 0.8163. Thus, the present value is € 250,000 × 0.8163 = € 204,075.

c)

Either € 2,000 invested has to be compounded and the value received has to be compared to € 3,000, or € 3,000 has to be discounted and the value received has to be compared to € 2,000.

Compound interest factor (4 years, 5 %): 1.2155; discount factor (4 years, 5 %): 0.8227

€ 2,000 € × 1.2155 = € 2,431.00 or 3,000 € × 0.8227 = € 2,468.10

We should see that in any case an amount of € 3,000 has the higher value at the end of year 4.

d)

Year	Current value	PVF	Present value
1	1,000	0.9259	925.90
2	2,000	0.8573	1,714.60
3	3,000	0.7938	2,381.40
Total			5,021.90

The grandfather would agree to give you € 5,021.90 'today'. The value of € 5,021.90 has to be understood as follows: No participant in the market would pay a higher value for these payments. No seller would agree to accept a lower value in case of a sale.

e)

$$€\ 20{,}000 \times \frac{1}{\text{PVA}} = €\ 20{,}000 \times \frac{1}{2.6730} = €\ 20{,}000 \times 0.3741 = €\ 7{,}482$$

Answer to exercise 3-2 Net present value method I

a)

A single investment is worthwhile if its net present value is positive. This means: NPV > 0. As far as deciding between mutually exclusive projects is concerned, then an investment 1 is better than an investment 2 if its net present value is greater. This means: $NPV_1 > NPV_2$.

3.8 Exercises with Answers

b)

	PVA	Alternative A		Alternative B	
		Current value	Present value	Current value	Present value
Initial outlay	1	-10,000	-10,000	-15,000	-15,000
Annuity	5.0757	2,100	10,659	3,100	15,735
Net present value			659		735

Alternative B is better because of the greater positive net present value.

Answer to exercise 3-3 Net present value method II

	PVA	Current value	Present value
Initial outlay	1	-35,000	-35,000
Annuity	7.9127	3,500	27,694
Net present value			-7,306

The net present value is € –7,306. This is the amount at which the investment outlay is not covered by cash flow. The investment is hence not a worthwhile project.

Answer to exercise 3-4 Net present value method III

Calculation of the net present values

	Land I	Land II	Land III
Sales value	80,000	60,000	175,000
Present value factor (4 %, 10 years)	0.6756	0.6756	0.6756
Discounted sales value	54,048	40,536	118,230
- Initial outlay	45,000	50,000	95,000
= Net present value	9,048	-9,464	23,230

Land II is rejected because of its negative net present value. Among land I and III choose the one with the larger positive net present value, thus land III.

Answer to exercise 3-5 Net present value method IV

a)

Offer 1:

Year	PVF	Advice	Current Value	Present value
1	1	Purchase price	10,200.00	10,200.00
Total				10,200.00

Offer 2:

Year	PVF	Advice	Current value	Present value
1	1	Leasing payment	2,400.00	2,400.00
2-5	3.6299		2,400.00	8,711.76
Total				11,111.76

Offer 3:

Year	PVF	Advice	Current value	Present value
1	1	Leasing payment	2,500.00	2,500.00
2	0.9615	Leasing payment	2,500.00	2,403.75
3	0.9246	Purchase price	5,200.00	4,807.92
Summe				9,711.67

The projects would have the following ranking: Offer 3 better than offer 1 better than offer 2. Since the comparison is based on cash outflow only, the offer with the lower value is preferred.

b)

Offer 1:

Year	PVF	Advice	Current value	Present value
1	1	Purchase price	10,200.00	10,200.00
Total				10,200.00

Offer 2:

Year	PVF/PVA	Advice	Current value	Present value
1	1	Leasing payment	2,400.00	2,400.00
2-5	3.1699		2,400.00	7,607.76
Total				10,007.76

Offer 3:

Year	PVF	Advice	Current value	Present value
1	1	Leasing payment	2,500.00	2,500.00
2	0.9091	Leasing payment	2,500.00	2,272.75
3	0.8264	Purchase price	5,200.00	4,297.28
Total				9,070.03

Repeating the exercise with a discount rate of 10 % yields the following ranking: Offer 3 better than offer 2 better than offer 1. It can be seen that the rank of the alternatives can change by varying the discount factor.

c)

Offer 1:

Year	PVF	Advice	Current value	Present value
1	0.8219	Purchase price	10,200.00	8,383.38
Total				8,383.38

Offer 2: No changes.

Offer 3: No changes.

The projects would have the following ranking: Offer 1 better than offer 3 better than offer 2.

Answer to exercise 3-6 Net present value method V

a)

Point in time	PVF	Cash inflows	Cash outflows	Cash flows	PV Cash flows
0	1.0000	0.00	11,200.00	-11,200.00	-11,200.00
1	0.9259	850.00	100.00	750.00	694.43
2	0.8573	850.00	100.00	750.00	642.98
3	0.7938	850.00	100.00	750.00	595.35
4	0.7350	850.00	100.00	750.00	551.25
5	0.6806	850.00	100.00	750.00	510.45
6	0.6302	850.00	100.00	750.00	472.65
7	0.5835	850.00	100.00	750.00	437.63
8	0.5403	850.00	100.00	750.00	405.23
9	0.5002	850.00	100.00	750.00	375.15
10	0.4632	850.00	100.00	750.00	347.40
NPV					-6,167.50

b)

Point in time	PVF	Cash inflows	Cash outflows	Cash flows	PV Cash flows
0	1.0000	0.00	0.00	0.00	0.00
1	0.9259	850.00	100.00	750.00	694.43
2	0.8573	850.00	100.00	750.00	642.98
3	0.7938	850.00	1,500.00	-650.00	-515.97
4	0.7350	850.00	1,500.00	-650.00	-477.75
5	0.6806	850.00	1,500.00	-650.00	-442.39
6	0.6302	850.00	1,500.00	-650.00	-409.63
7	0.5835	850.00	1,500.00	-650.00	-379.28
8	0.5403	850.00	1,500.00	-650.00	-351.20
9	0.5002	850.00	1,500.00	-650.00	-325.13
10	0.4632	850.00	1,500.00	-650.00	-301.08
NPV					-1,865.02

c)

Point in time	PVF	Cash inflows	Cash outflows	Cash flows	PV Cash flows
0	1.0000	0.00	0.00	0.00	0.00
1	0.9259	850.00	100.00	750.00	694.43
2	0.8573	850.00	100.00	750.00	642.98
3	0.7938	850.00	1,500.00	-650.00	-515.97
4	0.7350	850.00	1,500.00	-650.00	-477.75
5	0.6806	595.00	1,500.00	-905.00	-615.94
6	0.6302	595.00	1,500.00	-905.00	-570.33
7	0.5835	595.00	1,500.00	-905.00	-528.07
8	0.5403	595.00	1,500.00	-905.00	-488.97
9	0.5002	595.00	1,500.00	-905.00	-452.68
10	0.4632	595.00	1,500.00	-905.00	-419.20
NPV					-2,731.51

3.8 Exercises with Answers

d)

Point in time	PVF	Cash inflows	Cash outflows	Cash flows	PV Cash flows
0	1.0000	0.00	0.00	0.00	0.00
1	0.9259	850.00	100.00	750.00	694.43
2	0.8573	850.00	100.00	750.00	642.98
3	0.7938	850.00	1,500.00	-650.00	-515.97
4	0.7350	850.00	1,500.00	-650.00	-477.75
5	0.6806	850.00	1,500.00	-650.00	-442.39
6	0.6302	850.00	1,500.00	-650.00	-409.63
7	0.5835	850.00	1,500.00	-650.00	-379.28
8	0.5403	850.00	1,500.00	-650.00	-351.20
9	0.5002	850.00	1,500.00	-650.00	-325.13
10	0.4632	850.00	1,500.00	-650.00	-301.08
11	0.4289	850.00	100.00	750.00	321.68
12	0.3971	850.00	100.00	750.00	297.83
13	0.3677	850.00	100.00	750.00	275.78
14	0.3405	850.00	100.00	750.00	255.38
15	0.3152	850.00	100.00	750.00	236.40
16	0.2919	850.00	100.00	750.00	218.93
17	0.2703	850.00	100.00	750.00	202.73
18	0.2502	850.00	100.00	750.00	187.65
19	0.2317	850.00	100.00	750.00	173.78
20	0.2145	850.00	100.00	750.00	160.88
NPV					465.98

e) Not until the conditions are as advantageous as in subtask 'd', is the investment worthwhile. Then the net present value becomes positive.

Answer to exercise 3-7 Cost comparison method and net present value method

a)

	Model 1	Model 2	Model 3
Depreciation	12,000	14,000	16,000
Imputed interest	1,440	1,680	1,920
Operating costs	12,000	10,000	8,000
Other fixed costs	5,200	5,000	4,800
Total	30,640	30,680	30,720
Rank	1	2	3

According to the cost comparison method, model 1 has the lowest cost.

b)

The present values of cash outflows of each of the models are shown in the following table along with the ranking of each project on this basis.

	Model 1	Model 2	Model 3
Current value cash outflow	17,200	15,000	12,800
PVA 6 years, 4 %	5.2421	5.2421	5.2421
Present value cash outflow	90,164	78,632	67,099
+ Initial outlay	72,000	84,000	96,000
= Total present value cash outflow	162,164	162,632	163,099
Rank	1	2	3

Answer to exercise 3-8 Annuity method

	Land I	Land II	Land III
Sales value	80,000	60,000	175,000
PVF (4 %, 10 y.)	0.6756	0.6756	0.6756
Discounted sales value	54,048	40,536	118,230
- Initial outlay	45,000	50,000	95,000
= Net present value	9,048	-9,464	23,230
PVA (4 %, 10 y.)	8.1109	8.1109	8.1109
Annuity	1,116	-1,167	2,864

The ranking remains the same as with the net present value method.

Answer to exercise 3-9 Internal rate of return method

a)

First the net present values are calculated with discount rates of 4 % and 6 %.

Year	PVF 4 %	Current values cash flow	Present values cash flow
1	0.9615	0	0
2	0.9246	0	0
3	0.8890	20,000	17,780
4	0.8548	15,000	12,822
5	0.8219	40,000	32,876
Total			63,478
		Initial outlay	-60,000
		Net present value	3,478

3.8 Exercises with Answers

Year	PVF 6 %	Current values cash flow	Present values cash flow
1	0.9434	0	0
2	0.8900	0	0
3	0.8396	20,000	16,792
4	0.7921	15,000	11,882
5	0.7473	40,000	29,892
Total			58,566
		Initial outlay	-60,000
		Net present value	-1,435

The internal rate of return is calculated according to this formula:

$$i = i_1 - NPV_1 \frac{i_2 - i_1}{NPV_2 - NPV_1}$$

Substituting in the data of the example for discount rates of 4 % as well as 6 % gives:

$$i = 0.04 - €\,3,478 \frac{0.06 - 0.04}{€-1,434 - €\,3,478}$$

$$i = 0.04 - €\,3,478 \frac{0.02}{€ - 4,912}$$

$$i = 0.04 + \frac{69.56}{4,912}$$

$$i = 0.054 \text{ (rounded)}$$

Hence, the internal rate of return is 5.4 %.

b)

To start with the net present value is calculated with a discount rate of 10 %.

Year	PVF 10 %	Current values cash flow	Present values cash flow
1	0.9091	0	0
2	0.8264	0	0
3	0.7513	20,000	15,026
4	0.6830	15,000	10,245
5	0.6209	40,000	24,836
Total			50,107
		Initial outlay	-60,000
		Net present value	-9,893

3 Discounting Methods of Investment Appraisal

Again, substituting in the data of the example for discount rates of 4 % as well as 10 % gives:

$$i = 0.04 - €\,3{,}478 \; \frac{0.1 - 0.04}{€ - 9{,}893 - €\,3{,}478}$$

$$i = 0.04 - €\,3.478 \; \frac{0.06}{€ - 13{,}371}$$

$$i = 0.04 + \frac{208.68}{13{,}371}$$

$$i = 0.056 \text{ (rounded)}$$

Now, the internal rate of return is 5.6 %.

c)

To solve this problem you would set up the following Excel spreadsheet:

q	Present value year 1	Present value year 2	Present value year 3	Present value year 4	Present value year 5	Initial outlay	Net present value
1.0539	0	0	17,083.6	12,157.0	30,759.4	–60,000	0

The calculation based on Excel leads to an internal rate of return of 5.39 %. The interest rates calculated in parts a and b are only approximate solutions because they are the less accurate the more the interest rates used for the calculation differ from the actual internal rate of return.

d)

The internal rate of return decision criterion of 9 % suggests that the investment should be rejected.

Answer to exercise 3-10 Accounting rate of return method and internal rate of return method

a)

$$\text{Accounting rate of return} = \frac{\text{Average annual profit}}{\text{Average capital employed}} \times 100$$

The average annual profit is calculated as follows:

Additional revenues through the investment	€ 12,500
– Depreciation	€ 5,000
– Maintenance	€ 2,500
= Profit	€ 5,000

Average annual capital employed = $\dfrac{\text{Initial outlay}}{2} = \dfrac{€150{,}000}{2} = €\,75{,}000$

Calculation of the accounting rate of return: $\dfrac{€\,5{,}000}{€\,75{,}000} \times 100 = 6.7\,\%$

The investment is, therefore, worth undertaking.

b)

Revenues: 6,250 × € 2.00	€ 12,500
– Expenses	€ 2,500
= Annual cash flow	€ 10,000

$\text{PVA} = \dfrac{€\,150{,}000}{€\,10{,}000} = 15$

15.3725 is the nearest value in the table with the present value annuity factors. This gives an internal rate of return of 5 %.

c)

The accounting rate of return method shows a higher interest rate because this represents a value based on averages. The internal rate of return method however, values the cash flows of later years less. Therefore, the rate of return goes down and the investment is no longer worthwhile.

Answer to exercise 3-11 Non-discounting and discounting methods of investment appraisal

a)

Accounting rate of return = $\dfrac{\text{Average annual profit}}{\text{Average capital employed}} \times 100$

With an anticipated economic life of 20 years, we get the following annual depreciation rates: € 4,000 ÷ 20 years = € 200. Maintenance constitutes the variable costs.

The revenues are calculated as follows:
180 kWh per month at € 0.15 → 180 × 12 × € 0.15 = € 324.00.

The average annual profit is calculated as follows:

Revenues	€ 324.00
– Variable costs	€ 149.63
– Depreciation	€ 200.00
= Loss	€ 25.63

$$\text{Average annual capital employed} = \frac{\text{Initial outlay}}{2} = \frac{€\,4{,}000}{2} = €\,2{,}000$$

Consequently the accounting rate of return is: $\dfrac{€ - 25.63}{€\,2{,}000} \times 100 = -1.3\,\%$

The payback period is: $\dfrac{\text{Inital outlay}}{\text{average annual cash flow}} = \dfrac{€\,4{,}000}{€\,174.37} = 23$ years (rounded)

b)

We compile the results: The accounting rate of return is negative. Payback is longer than the asset's economic life. Therefore, the investment should be rejected.

c)

Due to the government grant the basis for calculating depreciation and average capital employed changes.

The average annual profit is then:

Revenues	€ 324.00
– Variable costs	€ 149.63
– Depreciation	€ 100.00
= Profit	€ 74.37

$$\text{Average annual capital employed} = \frac{\text{Initial outlay - government grant}}{2} = \frac{€\,2{,}000}{2} = €\,1{,}000.$$

Under the new conditions the accounting rate of return equals:

$\dfrac{€\,74.37}{€\,1{,}000} \times 100 = 7.4\,\%$

d)

The internal rate of return is calculated as follows:

$$PVA = \frac{\text{Present value of initial outlay}}{\text{Annuity}} = \frac{€\,2{,}000}{€\,174.37} = 11.4699$$

Hence, the internal rate of return is 6 %. This can be taken from the table of the annuity present value factors in the 20 year row.

Calculation of the net present value:

Annual cash flow: € 324.00 – € 149.63 = € 174.37

PVA (20 years, 6 %) 11.4699 × € 174.37 = € 2,000

Net present value = € 2,000 – € 2,000 = € 0

Even before calculating the net present value we saw that it must equal zero, because the internal rate of return is the discount factor which leads to a net present value of exactly zero.

e)

The explanation for the difference between the results is that discounting methods of investment appraisal account for the time value of money through the act of discounting. Future benefits are, therefore, less valuable with regard to the present which is the common reference point.

4 Investment Decision Making under Conditions of Uncertainty

4.1 Learning Objectives

By now you are well acquainted with the non-discounting and discounting methods of investment appraisal. Up until now, our analysis was based on calculations where the available data is certain. With non-ambiguous information, we calculated target values for the investment project, for instance the net present value, which gave us a single-value to decide whether the project was worth undertaking or not. In the following chapter we remove this assumption and explore whether there are investment appraisal techniques that support the decision maker reasonably even under conditions of uncertainty. If you take into consideration that capital expenditures are long-term investments which bind capital over a long period of time, then it is rather unrealistic to assume that the future cash flow of a project can be estimated with accuracy. Even the initial outlay can be subject to estimate errors. Uncertainty over the state of the economy might result in possible losses from each investment project. Thus, in this chapter

- you will first become acquainted with the methodological basics and the structure of decision situations.
- As in the previous chapters we stick to the basic decision situation of the car sharing company.
- We discuss four different methods which lead to recommendations in decision-making even under risk. These four methods are the correction method, sensitivity analysis, risk analysis und the decision tree.
- As in the chapters about non-discounting and discounting methods of investment appraisal, you will learn the strengths and the weaknesses of these methods.
- A Summary and evaluation as well as exercises with their solutions will conclude the chapter.

4.2 Uncertainty and Risk

In the previous chapters the data employed to decide whether an investment is profitable or not was certain. From now on, we will consider that reality is uncertain. Decision makers are not entirely uninformed, in that they expect a certain cash flow from the investment, but are aware that the actual outcome may differ from what was expected. Next, it is difficult to predict the life of the investment precisely. Furthermore, it is nearly impossible to project the cash flow at the end the anticipated average life of the investment exactly. The longer the time horizon, the more difficult it is to make useful estimates. Uncertain input data lead to uncertain final results. Calculated net present values won't be reached with certainty. If you don't take into account the risk of an investment, then the net present value suggests a certainty with regard to the investment's profitability which is false and misleading.

Whereas purchase cost for the investment can be considered as nearly certain, because it has to be paid promptly, the cash inflows depend greatly on economic trends and on the possible emergence of competition in the relevant market. Future cash outflows depend on the development of energy cost, changes in currency exchange rates or wages. The discount factor itself has to be estimated. Thus the input depends on the economic environment and lead to different outcomes depending on realised external conditions.

We assume the superiority of the net present value approach, because this is the most exact method in assessing whether an investment project is worthwhile or not. Then we make reference to conditions where cash flows are no longer known with certainty. Of course, we could also make use of the presented techniques available to the decision maker under uncertainty for the other methods of investment appraisal.

In managerial decision theory the following terminology is used for decisions under uncertainty:

- Frequency: We have to distinguish singular decisions from those often repeated from an identical starting position.[16]

- Knowledge over probabilities of an occurrence of certain data: A distinction has to be made, whether the probability of an occurrence is known (risk) or not (uncertainty).[17] If probabilities for the occurrence are known, this enables us to deal with risk in a more analytical way. For known probabilities of outcomes we can make a further distinction between objective or subjective probabilities. Objective probability can be measured. Subjective probability is an estimate.

---

[16] Cf. Adam, Dietrich, Investitionscontrolling, 3rd ed., München 2000, p. 334.

[17] Cf. Wöhe, Günter, Einführung in die Allgemeine Betriebswirtschaftslehre, 22th ed., München 2005, p. 114.

In practice, the distinction between risk and uncertainty does not seem to be of great importance. The term risk is used in everyday conversation to refer to any situation involving the possibility of an undesired outcome, whether or not possibilities are known. Furthermore, there is hardly ever a real-world environment in which probabilities are known with certainty. Most past decisions are non-repeatable and, therefore, accurate derivation of probabilities is not possible. That is why we will use risk and uncertainty in this book in a more general sense. In the following, only those methods are presented which help to assess investment projects under risk in practice.[18]

4.3 Correction Method

4.3.1 Introduction

A simple and somehow intuitive approach to uncertainty is made by the correction method. When using the correction method, uncertainty is implemented through risk-adjusted input variables.

The steps in the analysis are:

1. Correction of input data through risk-adjustments after the principle of caution.

2. After the correction of the input data the project's net present value is recalculated.

3. We will perform only the investment projects which still yield a positive net present value after the correction.

First we must clarify what the input variables of an investment appraisal are. These are:

- the employed discount rate,
- the estimated cash inflow, including possible salvage values,
- the estimated cash outflow and
- the anticipated average life.

---

[18] For other methods of investment appraisal under conditions of uncertainty cf. Kruschwitz, Lutz, Investitionsrechnung, op. cit., pp. 297-453.

Table 4-1 reveals how a recalculation of the net present value can be made with more sensitivity to the input data.

Table 4-1: Correction of the input variables

Input variable	Correction of the input variable
Interest rate	Raise
Estimated cash inflow	Reduction
Estimated cash outflow	Raise
Anticipated average life	Shortening

The higher the uncertainty, the more we should correct the values of the key project variables.

4.3.2 Comparison of Alternatives

We go back to the application of the net present value method to the investment of the car sharing company. This table was shown in Chapter 3 is repeated here as Table 4-2 for convenience. The SM Samurai represented the better investment because its net present value is higher at the amount of € 3,298.

Table 4-2 Initial data for the comparison of alternatives

	AK Rasant	SM Samurai
Initial outlay	9,000	14,000
Present value of an annuity	1.8594	2.7232
Annual cash outflow	9,750	9,750
Annual cash inflow	17,150	17,850
Net present value	4,760	8,058
Difference between net present values		3,298

Now, after a carefully made estimate, we correct the annual cash inflow and the annual cash outflow and start recalculating the projects' net present values in Table 4-3. We raise the projects' annual cash outflow by € 1,000 to € 10,750. We lower the projects' annual cash inflow of € 0.49 per kilometre for the AK Rasant and € 0.51 per kilometre for the SM Samurai by € 0.01 per kilometre. The discount rate is still 5 %.

4.3 Correction Method

Table 4-3 Net present values for the comparison of alternatives using the correction method

	AK Rasant	SM Samurai
Initial outlay	9,000	14,000
Present value of an annuity	1.8594	2.7232
Annual cash outflow	10,750	10,750
Annual cash inflow	16,800	17,500
Net present value	2,249	4,382
Difference between net present values		2,132

The net present value of the SM Samurai now equals € 4,382; it exceeds the net present value of the AK Rasant by € 2,132. Therefore, we find that we still prefer the SM Samurai. Thereby, we left the purchase price as well as the discount rate unchanged.

4.3.3 Evaluation of the Correction Method

1. The correction method takes into consideration a possible risk aversion of the investor.

2. The correction method can be used easily and can be communicated without any problems.

3. Applying the correction method forces the decision makers to weigh the encompassing risk explicitly.

4. The greater the uncertainty, the more the key project variables have to be corrected.

5. There is no exact way to determine to what extent the several corrections have to be made. The dimension of the adjustment cannot be calculated exactly. It has to be done individually.

6. You have to weigh very carefully, which input data should be corrected. If you don't, the cumulation of the diverse corrections will lead to an overly negative assessment of the investment project.

7. This method can be used reasonably for smaller investment projects which do not justify extensive corporate planning. For bigger investment projects the method is not precise enough.

4.4 Sensitivity Analysis

4.4.1 Introduction

Sensitivity analysis is a means that looks for answers to the following questions: What is the impact of changing the value of an input variable on the final result and does it change the ranking of investment alternatives with regard to their profitability?

We can follow two basic problems:

1. If the investor already has an idea about the band width of the project's sensitive variables, then he moves through their optimistic and pessimistic levels to determine which variables cause the greatest impact on the on the net present value. Scenario analyses show what happens to the net present value when we ask 'what if' questions: What if the sales are considerably lower than expected?

2. Alternatively, after having chosen the uncertain input variables, the investor could calculate the so-called critical variables. Critical values are variables which may change the profitability of an investment project. We already performed such calculations within the non-discounting methods while deriving critical values for the investment's capacity. In this case the critical value is the one for which the net present value remains positive if an income variable falls or a cost variable rises.

4.4.2 Comparison of Alternatives

Again we go back to our example by applying the net present value method to the comparison of alternatives. The same example was used in the previous chapter to exemplify the correction method. Here again we refer to this example to illustrate the particularities of the sensitivity analysis. We start with a scenario analysis test.

Table 4-4 refers to the data basis with certainty which is now regarded as the most likely value estimated for the input variables:

Table 4-4 Data basis for the comparison of alternatives

	AK Rasant	SM Samurai
Initial outlay	9,000	14,000
Present value of an annuity	1.8594	2.7232
Annual cash flow	7,400	8,100
Net present value	4,760	8,058
Difference between net present values		3,298

4.4 Sensitivity Analysis

We analyse how the net present value changes, if we

- raise the cash flow by 20 % for one thing (Table 4-5) and
- reduce the cash flow by 20 % for another thing (Table 4-6).[19]

Table 4-5: Rise of cash flow by 20 % within the sensitivity analysis

	AK Rasant	SM Samurai
Initial outlay	9,000	14,000
Present value of an annuity	1.8594	2.7232
Annual cash flow	8,880	9,720
Net present value	7,511	12,470
Difference between net present values		4,958

The net present value of the SM Samurai rises from € 8,058 to € 12,470.

Table 4-6: Reduction of cash flow by 20 % within the sensitivity analysis

	AK Rasant	SM Samurai
Initial outlay	9,000	14,000
Present value of an annuity	1.8594	2.7232
Annual cash flow	5,920	6,480
Net present value	2,008	3,646
Difference between net present values		1,639

The net present value of the SM Samurai falls from € 8,058 to € 3,646.

Table 4-7: Synopsis of the results of the band width analysis

	AK Rasant	SM Samurai
Initial net present value	€ 4,760	€ 8,058
Net present value with higher cash flow	€ 7,511	€ 12,470
Net present value with lower cash flow	€ 2,008	€ 3,646

---

[19] See Dayananda, Don, et al., Capital Budgeting: Financial Appraisal of Investment Projects, Cambridge 2002, pp. 136-141 for considerations about the selection of variables for sensitivity analysis.

Table 4-7 reveals that even a band width of 20 % regarding cash flows does not change the fact that the investment as a whole is advantageous. According to this the investment stays favourable even in consideration of risk. In any case the SM Samurai remains preferable.

Another approach we consider asks for the so-called critical values. The break-even analysis endeavours to find the values of input data, which lead to any positive net present value. In this case one could ask how far the cash flow could fall so that the net present value just does not become negative.

Therefore, we choose the general formula for calculating the net present value. This is:

Net present value = present value cash inflow – present value cash inflow

We got the net present value for the SM Samurai from the following equation:

Net present value = [(€ 0.51 – € 0.17) × 35,000 – € 3,800] · PVA (3 years, 5 %) – € 14,000

Net present value = € 8,100 × 2.7232 – € 14,000

Net present value = € 8,058

For the cash flows we don't take concrete numbers, but variables. In this case we assume that the number of kilometres driven is uncertain. Then we assume the equation being zero. By solving for the number of kilometres in the following equation we get:

0 = [(€ 0.51 – € 0.17) × number km – € 3,800] × PVA (3 years, 5 %) – € 14,000

0 = [€ 0.34 × number km – € 3,800] × 2.7232 – € 14,000

0 = € 0.925888 × number km – 10,348.16 € – € 14,000

0 = € 0.925888 × number km – € 24,348.16

€ 24,348.16 = € 0.925888 × number km

Number km = 26,297

Per period they have to sell at least 26,297 kilometres to make sure that the net present value does not turn negative. In other words: If the number of kilometres is 24.9 % less than estimated, then the project is no longer profitable.

Another application of this method is to vary the discount factor. For example, one could ask how much we could raise the interest rate without getting a negative net present value. This is, by definition, the internal rate of return, because the internal rate of return is the critical value for the input variable interest rate. We already calculated the internal rate of return in Chapter 3.5.2 and thereby solved another question in the context of the sensitivity analysis.

4.4 Sensitivity Analysis

The discount rate can rise from 5 % to 34 %, an increase of 580 %, to reach the break even point.

Similarly, the anticipated life of the SM Samurai would have to fall to 1.85 years before the project has a negative net present value. If operating expenses are 49.7 % above the estimated figure, the project will have a negative net present value. Table 4-8 shows the results if this procedure is repeated for each of the figures in the net present value analysis. In doing so, we can identify the figures to which the project is most sensitive. While carrying out these calculations the other estimates are held at their original best-estimate level. The figures suggest that the number of kilometres driven is most important followed by the anticipated life.

Table 4-8 Identifying the SM Samurai's sensitive input variables

Input variable	Original best estimate	Critical value	Percentage change
Amount of km	35,000	26,297	-24.9
Anticipated life in years	3	1.85	-38.3
Discount rate in %	5	34	580.0
Operating expenses per kilometre in €	0.17	0.25	49.7

We should conclude from this that the car sharing company's management should monitor the most sensitive estimates very carefully. But is does not give a clear rule to guide the decision maker as to how he or she should react.

4.4.3 Evaluation of the Sensitivity Analysis

1. Sensitivity analysis gives a quick answer to the question 'what can go wrong?' Probabilities need not to be estimated, and the key drivers of success of an investment can easily be identified.

2. Sensitivity analysis provides insights into the sensitivity of the net present value to variations of the most sensitive input variables.

3. The procedure can be easily understood and communicated.

4. With the aid of the sensitivity analysis, the decision maker can identify the areas of the investment project which should be of most concern. Furthermore, he can determine whether it is important to gather further information in these areas.

5. As with the correction method, it is not possible to determine exactly how much the input variables should be corrected. This decision has to be made individually.

6. Scenario analysis allows presenting pessimistic and optimistic scenarios as 'best case' or 'worst case' outcomes.

7. Sensitivity analyses show if there is a considerable amount of risk, but they suffer from shortcomings. There is no clear indication of how the choice of an investment opportunity should be made. In addition, it allows for change of variables only one at a time.

4.5   Risk Analysis

4.5.1   Introduction

So far, we identified two simple means of dealing with risk and uncertainty. In the following subchapter we explore a means which provides the decision maker with more information and, therefore, a better understanding of the factors which affect the investment project's cash flow. Furthermore, it allows changing more than only one variable at a time. Risk analysis or Monte Carlo simulation, due to the historical association of roulette wheels, is a simulation concept which means developing a model and then conducting experiments on a computer using that model. It aims at simulating how the real world would behave under certain circumstances. The task of the risk analysis is to derive a probability distribution of the project's net present value.[20] We arrive at a risk profile of the investment and not at a single net present value as point estimate.

These are the steps into which the risk analysis process can be divided:

1. Selection of the uncertain input variables.

2. Estimate of the probability distributions of the uncertain input variables.

3. Allocation and generation of random numbers for the uncertain input variables.

4. Calculation of the output variable.

5. Calculation of the relative frequencies of the net present value and derivation of a risk profile.

6. Analysis of the results, decision on the investment project.

---

[20] For reasons of clearness we limit the analysis to simulation models. For a risk analysis based on analytical methods cf. Pflaumer, Peter, Investitionsrechnung, 5th ed., München 2004, pp. 144-153.

4.5.2 Comparison of Alternatives

Again, we refer to the example from the comparison of alternatives from the net present value method with certainty. We explain the SM Samurai, because its net present value exceeds the value of the AK Rasant. Now, we perform the above mentioned steps.

- To 1) Selection of the uncertain input variables

  Both, the discount rate as well as the initial capital cost are regarded as controllable. But in our case we identify cash flows depending on the market demand and the useful life expectancy as uncertain input data. For the cash flows from the investment project we work with the same values as we did within the sensitivity analysis (Table 4-9). With respect to the anticipated life instead of a best-guess estimate of only three years, we assume a fluctuation margin of two to four years.

Table 4-9 Definition of the uncertain input variables

Cash flow	€ 6,480/€ 8,100/€ 9,720
Anticipated average life	2 to 4 years

- To 2) Estimate of the probability distributions of the uncertain input variables

  We set up a range of values and allocate probability weights to it. We assume that cash flows reach the certain value of € 8,100 only with a probability of 40 %. With a probability of 40 %, cash flows are € 6,480. With a probability of 20 %, we select a higher cash flow of € 9,720. In practice, there will be a whole distribution of possible outcomes for each input variable.

  With regard to the investment's life, the anticipated average life under certainty, three years, is reached with a 50 % probability. The possibility that the car can be used only for two years is reached with a 20 % probability. With a 30 % probability we expect that the car's useful life to be four years. Table 4-10 contains the data.

Table 4-10 Probability distributions of the uncertain input variables

Cash flow in €	6,480	8,100	9,720
Probability	0.4	0.4	0.2
Anticipated average life	2 years	3 years	4 years
Probability	0.2	0.5	0.3

4 Investment Decision Making under Conditions of Uncertainty

- To 3) Allocation and generation of random numbers for the uncertain input variables

Step 3 aims at generating the values for the critical input variables which are used in step 4 to derive the net present value. As can be seen, the input variables are no longer given as before, but are selected with the aid of a computer simulation model. In Table 4-11 the random numbers from 1 to 10 are allocated to the uncertain input data according to the probabilities from step 2.

Table 4-11 Allocation of random numbers to the uncertain input data

Cash flow in €	6,480	8,100	9,720
Allocated random number	1, 2, 3, 4	5, 6, 7, 8	9, 10
Life	2 years	3 years	4 years
Allocated random number	1, 2	3, 4, 5, 6, 7	8, 9, 10

Then the allocation of random numbers to the single parameter values of the uncertain input data is carried out. This comes about as with dice, a coin or as setting up a roulette wheel by a random-number generator. A simulation run, replicate or iteration can be compared with the concept of a toss of dice. This is illustrated in Figure 4-1.

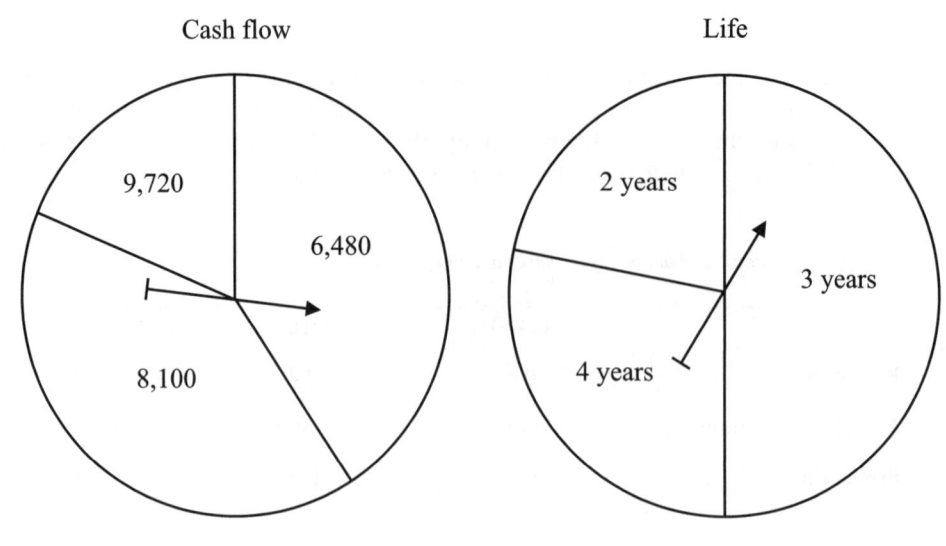

Figure 4-1 Monte Carlo Simulation to incorporate probability distributions of cash flows and economic life

4.5 Risk Analysis

We assume that the simulation has generated the random numbers in Table 4-12.

Table 4-12 Generated random numbers for the uncertain input data

Replicate	1	2	3	4	5	6	7	8
Random number for cash flow	7	5	10	4	7	10	9	3
Random number for life	3	6	7	3	8	5	4	2

Using the input variables generated in this manner, we will now calculate the net present value.

- To 4) Calculation of the output variable

In Table 4-13 we calculate the output variable 'net present value'. For each replicate we calculate the net present value estimates based on the input data cash flow and life corresponding to the random numbers from step 3.

Table 4-13 Net present values for the iterations

Replicate	Cash flow	Life	PVA	Net present value
1	8,100	3	2.7232	8,058
2	8,100	3	2.7232	8,058
3	9,720	3	2.7232	12,470
4	6,480	3	2.7232	3,646
5	8,100	4	3.5460	14,723
6	9,720	3	2.7232	12,470
7	9,720	3	2.7232	12,470
8	6,480	2	1.8594	-1,951

The net present value estimates range between € –1,951 und € 14,723. As we can see, the net present value of € 8,058, calculated under the conditions of certainty, is derived for only two of a total of eight simulation runs.

- To 5) Calculation of the relative frequencies of the net present value and derivation of a risk profile

In Table 4-14, we start with the highest value and finish with the lowest of the net present value to derive its relative frequencies and its cumulative relative frequencies. The cumulative relative frequencies describe the net present value's distribution function. Here, we run only eight simulations to keep the calculation simple and understandable. In practice, the model is run a number of times more to get a large number of net present value outcomes. You must run as many simulation runs as necessary until there are no or only marginal changes with regard to the net present value's distribution. This makes the data more reliable.

Table 4-14: Results of the risk analysis

Net present value in €	Relative frequency	Cumulative relative frequency
14,723	0.125	0.125
12,470	0.375	0.500
8,058	0.250	0.750
3,646	0.125	0.875
−1,951	0.125	1.000

The computed net present values are used to plot a risk profile in Figure 4-2. For that purpose the values are transferred into a co-ordinate system. Along the horizontal axis the net present values are recorded, along the vertical axis the cumulative relative frequencies.

Figure 4-2 Risk profile

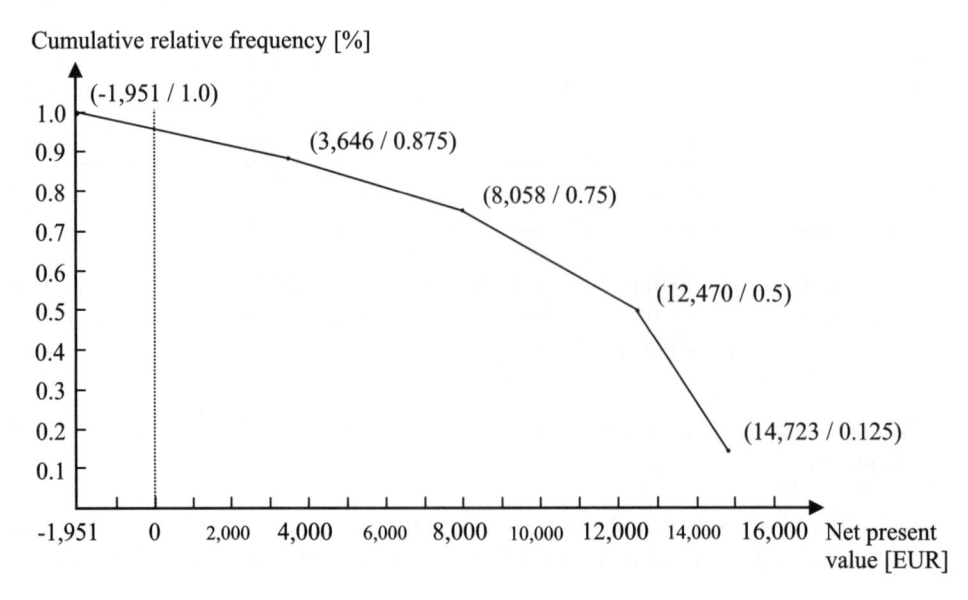

- To 6) Analysis of the results, decision on the investment project

For each net present value along the horizontal axis, the vertical axis indicates the probability that the net present value will be this value. It appears that the net present value is positive with a probability of 87.5 %. Therefore we can assume that the investment project is rather worthwhile, because with a probability of only 12.5 %, we must accept negative net present values.

4.5.3 Evaluation of the Risk Analysis

1. If we compare the risk analysis with the methods under uncertainty, which we discussed first, the sensitivity analysis and the correction method, then the risk analysis is more precise and gives decision makers a more detailed view of risk. The relevance of uncertainty becomes evident through the cumulative percentage of the net present value.

2. Chances and risks of the investment become clear.

3. Risk analysis takes into consideration both certain and uncertain input variables. It allows changes in several variables simultaneously.

4. The probability distributions of the uncertain input variables are estimated subjectively. This holds a first source of error. But the results of a risk analysis are, of course, more reliable than those of a single guess as by the correction method.

5. Keep in mind that the net present value is derived from sampling, not from a precise knowledge.

6. Simulation techniques are most appropriate when considering large projects because they are time consuming and expensive.

7. It is problematic to assume that the probability distributions of the uncertain variables are constant over time. But with the decision tree analysis we can allow for variable probabilities. In the following section we will introduce this technique.

4.6 Decision Tree Analysis

4.6.1 Introduction

Continuing from the discussion of the previous subchapters let us now look more closely at another advanced solution to the problems caused by uncertainty. The decision tree approach to investment decision making refers to situations where sequential decisions are concerned. Multi-level decision alternatives are clearly shown graphically and brought into a logical structure. Temporary interdependencies between the initial decision and subsequent decisions depending on possible states of the economy are taken into consideration. These sequential decisions are e.g. decisions about asset expansion projects, abandonment decisions or decisions within the marketing mix like price changes or the launching of advertising measures.

We tackle uncertainty by fixed planning as well as by flexible planning. The difference is that flexible planning works with conditional plans. Sequential decision making allows for starting small and then expanding if demand is sufficient. For investors this has the advantage of checking on the market to determine if planned demand can be realised. The reader must be careful not to be misled here. The adjustment of decisions to the development of the state of the economy is not unusual in business. The particularity of flexible planning (Chapter 4.6.3) lies in considering the consequences of the possible sequential decisions *before* the initial investment in period 0. The future adjustments are virtually anticipated to find an optimal sequence of decisions over time. The optimisation starts at the right-hand side and works backward, choosing the optimal decision at each decision node.

By contrast we examine fixed planning (Chapter 4.6.2) which has no conditional plans. However this approach considers only part of all available action alternatives. This may lead to a sub-optimal investment decision. Therefore, one could object that such a procedure is therefore a priori tainted with such imperfections that presenting this approach is not worthwhile at all. At this stage we can respond that flexible planning will generate better results but demands more extensive planning. Fixed planning may allow finding a solution for an investment decision with economically justifiable effort. As in other areas of business management we have to balance accuracy on one side and costs of planning on the other.

4.6.2 Comparison of Alternatives: Fixed Planning

To perform the fixed planning approach, we complete the following steps:

1. The estimated data of the investment alternatives are presented with the aid of a tree as a consequence of decisions.

2. A decision tree has decision nodes, probability nodes and outcome nodes.

3. Decision nodes mark the investor's action alternatives. They are represented by squares.

4.6 Decision Tree Analysis

4. The round probability nodes determine the state of the economy for the investor's business. The sum of the probabilities at the dashed branches equals exactly one.

5. In the decision nodes as well as in the probability nodes lines branch out.

6. The results of the investment (e.g. total cost, total profit, rates of return or net present values) are presented in the outcome nodes.

7. Now we choose the alternative which maximises the expected net present value in t_0. This implies the assumption that investors behave risk neutral.

In the case under consideration we must find if the expected net present value of the AK Rasant or that of the SM Samurai is higher. As with the approaches of investment appraisal presented so far, we refer to the data from the comparison of alternatives using the net present value approach. Table 4-15 repeats the initial data:

Table 4-15 Initial data for the comparison of alternatives using the fixed planning

	AK Rasant	SM Samurai
Initial outlay	9,000	14,000
PVA	1.8594	2.7232
Annual cash flow	7,400	8,100
Net present value	4,760	8,058
Difference between net present values		3,298

In the decision point t_0 the original decision has to be taken.[21] Either the investor chooses alternative 1 (AK Rasant) or alternative 2 (SM Samurai). The cash flows in periods 1 and 2 relate to whether the economy is in a recessional state or is booming. We assume that the decision makers in the car sharing company are optimistic with regard to the development of the economic situation. They estimate the following probabilities for the state of the economy:

Period 1	$p(h_1) = 0.7$
	$p(l_1) = 0.3$
Period 2	$p(h_2/h_1) = 0.7$; $p(l_2/h_1) = 0.3$
	$p(h_2/l_1) = 0.3$; $p(l_2/l_1) = 0.7$

---

[21] According to Blohm, Hans, Klaus Lüder and Christina Schaefer, Investition, 9th ed., München 2006, pp. 263-269.

4 Investment Decision Making under Conditions of Uncertainty

This can be shown is a tree of probabilities (Figure 4-3). Then the lines branching out from the node represent probabilities for each state of the economy (boom or recession).

Figure 4-3 Probability tree

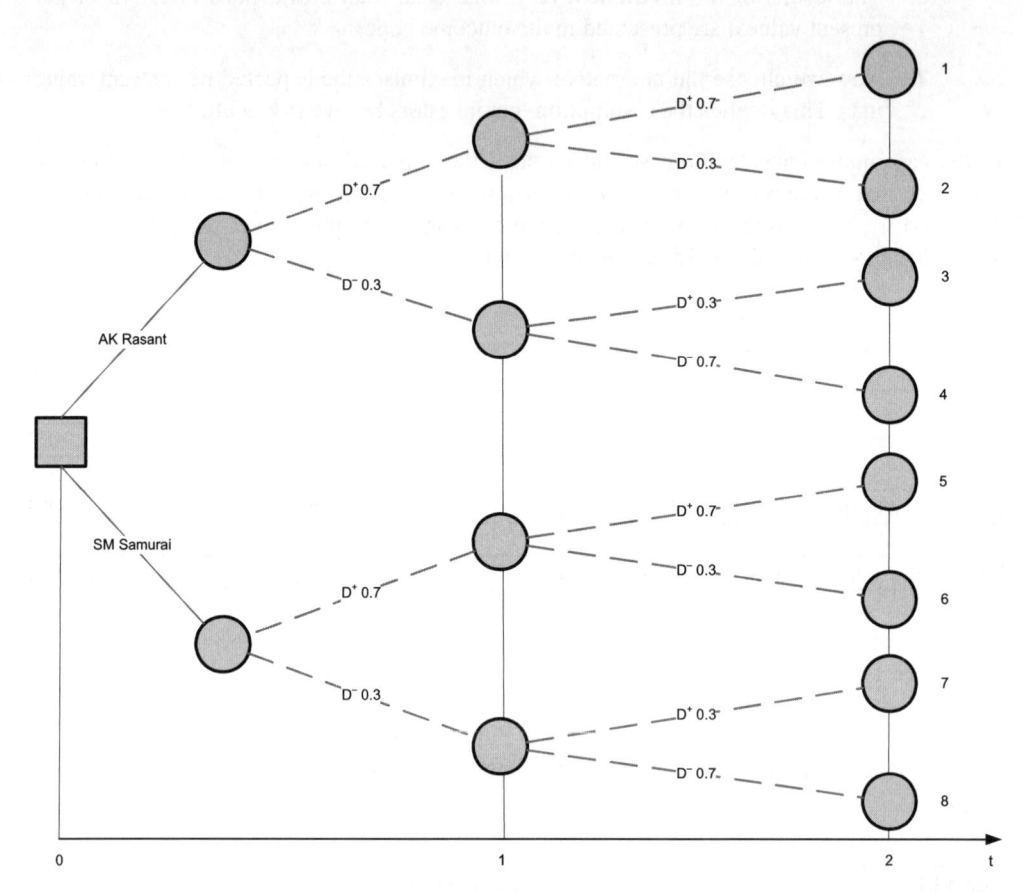

We can see that there are exactly four possible ways to a final node in period 2 after having made a decision for one of the cars. The probability for each way can be calculated by multiplying the probabilities of a single outcome to occur. For instance, the probability for a boom in both periods (final node 1) is 0.7 × 0.7 = 0.49. For the other final nodes the probabilities can be calculated this way.

In Table 4-16, we estimate the cash flow from the investment. On one side we use the value with which we have been working in the standard net present value approach. In this case, this is the value for a booming economy. For a recession we reduce these values by 20 %. In our car sharing company we assumed an economic life of two years for the AK Rasant and of three years for the SM Samurai. To reach comparability, we assume that the SM Samurai

4.6 Decision Tree Analysis

can be sold after two years at its book value. That is a current value of € 4,667.[22] This value is integrated into the calculations at the point of time t_2 by augmenting the cash flow for period 2 at exactly this amount.

Table 4-16 Current value of cash flows from the investment depending on the state of the economy

	Current value cash flow in period 1		Current value cash flow in period 2	
	Boom	Recession	Boom	Recession
AK Rasant	7,400	5,920	7,400	5,920
SM Samurai	8,100	6,480	12,767	11,147

To keep the decision tree clearly laid out and to facilitate its calculation, the current values of cash flows are discounted in Table 4-17 to the decision point of time t_0.

Table 4-17 Discounted cash flows from the investment project depending on the state of the economy

	Present value cash flow in period 1		Present value cash flow in period 2	
	Boom	Recession	Boom	Recession
AK Rasant	7,048	5,638	6,712	5,370
SM Samurai	7,714	6,171	11,580	10,111

The decision problem management is facing is summarised in Figure 4-4. In period 1 there is an outcome from the investment. This is the expected cash flow. The firm believes that the cash flows will be determined by the overall state of the economy. Therefore, there is a probability node before the outcome of period 1. If the demand turns out to be favourable, then a cash flow of € 7,048 can be reached. If demand turns out to be unfavourable a cash flow of € 5,638 can be reached. The further description of the decision tree starts in period 1 in the upper node, that is, we start with the assumption of having chosen alternative 1 in period 0 and that the demand turns out to be favourable in period 1. In period 2 again the demand can come out favourable (cash flow € 6,712, node 1) or unfavourable (cash flow € 5,370, node 2). For the nodes 3 to 8 the figures are calculated this way.

---

[22] Initial outlay of € 14,000 ÷ 3 years = € 4,667 depreciation per year.

128   4 Investment Decision Making under Conditions of Uncertainty

Figure 4-4 Decision tree – fixed planning

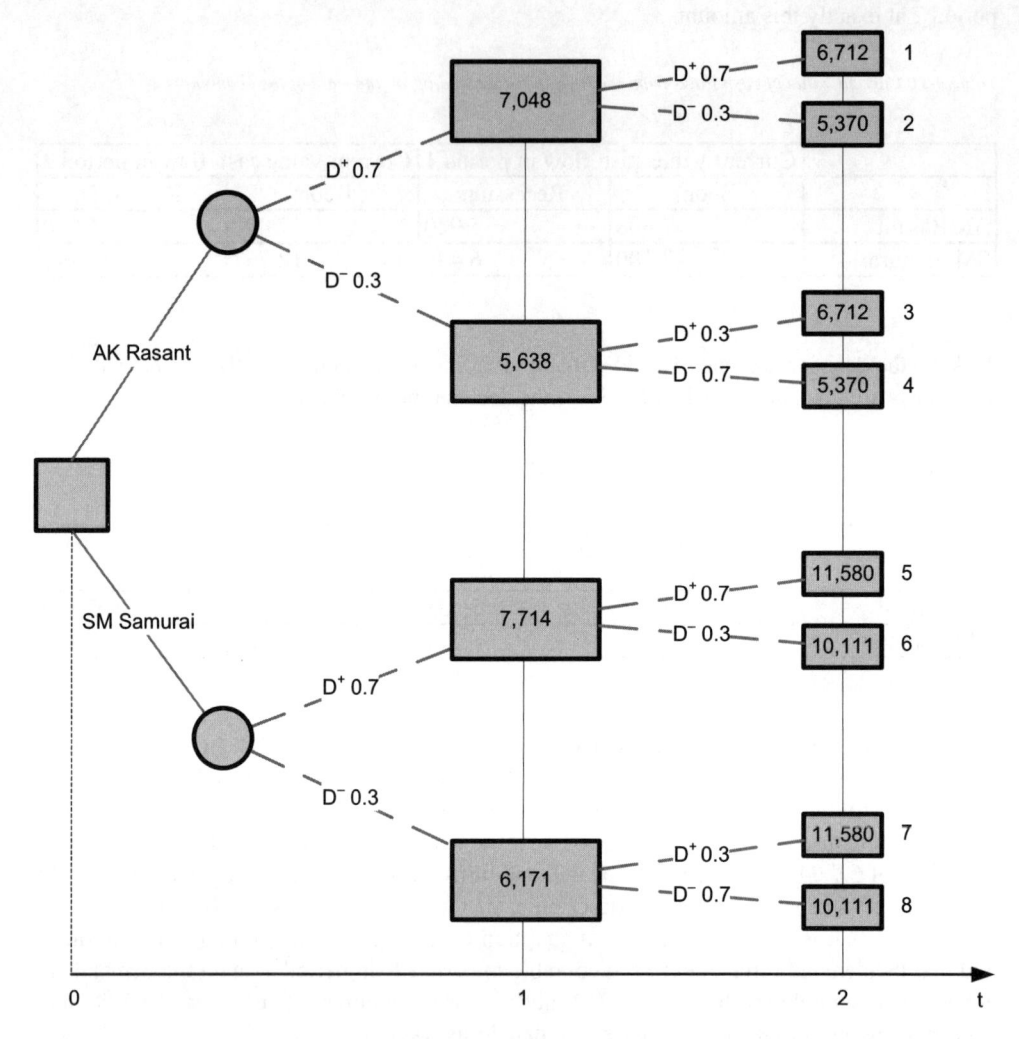

[Decision tree diagram]

AK Rasant branch:
- D⁺ 0.7 → 7,048 → D⁺ 0.7 → 6,712 (1); D⁻ 0.3 → 5,370 (2)
- D⁻ 0.3 → 5,638 → D⁺ 0.3 → 6,712 (3); D⁻ 0.7 → 5,370 (4)

SM Samurai branch:
- D⁺ 0.7 → 7,714 → D⁺ 0.7 → 11,580 (5); D⁻ 0.3 → 10,111 (6)
- D⁻ 0.3 → 6,171 → D⁺ 0.3 → 11,580 (7); D⁻ 0.7 → 10,111 (8)

Time axis: 0, 1, 2, t

In Table 4-18 we compute the weighted net present values and the expected net present values for the outcome nodes in period 2.[23]

---

[23] The net present value in node 1 is exactly the same as the one which we derived for the AK Rasant using the net present value method with certainty. Here, this represents only one of four possible outcomes in the final nodes for the AK Rasant. The values for the SM Samurai cannot be compared to those of our earlier calculation, because now we refer to a time horizon of only two periods. The expected net present value is calculated as arithmetic mean: $\sum_{i=1}^{n} p_i \times NPV_i$.

4.6 Decision Tree Analysis

Table 4-18 Net present values and weighted net present values in the outcome nodes of period 2 using the fixed planning approach

Outcome	Initial outlay	PV CF in period 1	PV CF in period 2	Net present value	Probability	Weighted net present value
Node 1	-9,000	7,048	6,712	4,760	0.49	2,332.40
Node 2	-9,000	7,048	5,370	3,418	0.21	717.78
Node 3	-9,000	5,638	6,712	3,350	0.09	301.50
Node 4	-9,000	5,638	5,370	2,008	0.21	421.68
Expected net present value for the AK Rasant						3,773.36
Node 5	-14,000	7,714	11,580	5,294	0.49	2,594.06
Node 6	-14,000	7,714	10,111	3,825	0.21	803.25
Node 7	-14,000	6,171	11,580	3,751	0.09	337.59
Node 8	-14,000	6,171	10,111	2,282	0.21	479.22
Expected net present value for the SM Samurai						4,214.12

The expected net present value of each vehicle is calculated by adding the weighted net present values in the final nodes. It is therefore profitable to buy the SM Samurai because of its higher expected net present value of € 4,214.12. In the next section we will perform the flexible planning approach with the same basic data. Then we will check if other consequences occur for the decisions makers to deal with.

4.6.3 Comparison of Alternatives: Flexible Planning

Using the flexible planning approach we consider further decision strategies. As can be seen from Table 4-19 we use identical initial data as with the fixed planning for the comparison of alternatives. Again the cash flows in periods 1 and 2 depend on the development of demand, either favourable or unfavourable.

Table 4-19 Discounted cash flows from the investment project depending on the state of the economy

	Present value cash flow in period 1		Present value cash flow in period 2	
	Boom	Recession	Boom	Recession
AK Rasant	7,048	5,638	6,712	5,370
SM Samurai	7,714	6,171	11,580	10,111

The flexible planning has the particularity that consecutive decisions can be taken into account. After period 1 the investor can react to the state of the economy to determine the most advantageous further steps. Thereto we undertake the following considerations:

- In period 1 the investment project can be continued as planned without any strategic changes.

- If demand turns out to be unfavourable, then a marketing campaign can be launched to develop the sales figures. We expect the costs of this campaign to be € 300. That is, as for the cash flows, the previously discounted value to period t_0.

In comparison to fixed planning there are eight further decision options whose ensuing decisions are dependent upon the development of the state of the economy in the first period. The probabilities for the state of the economy remain unchanged. If the company launches a marketing campaign, then the probability for high demand is 0.8.

Figure 4-5 Decision tree – flexible planning

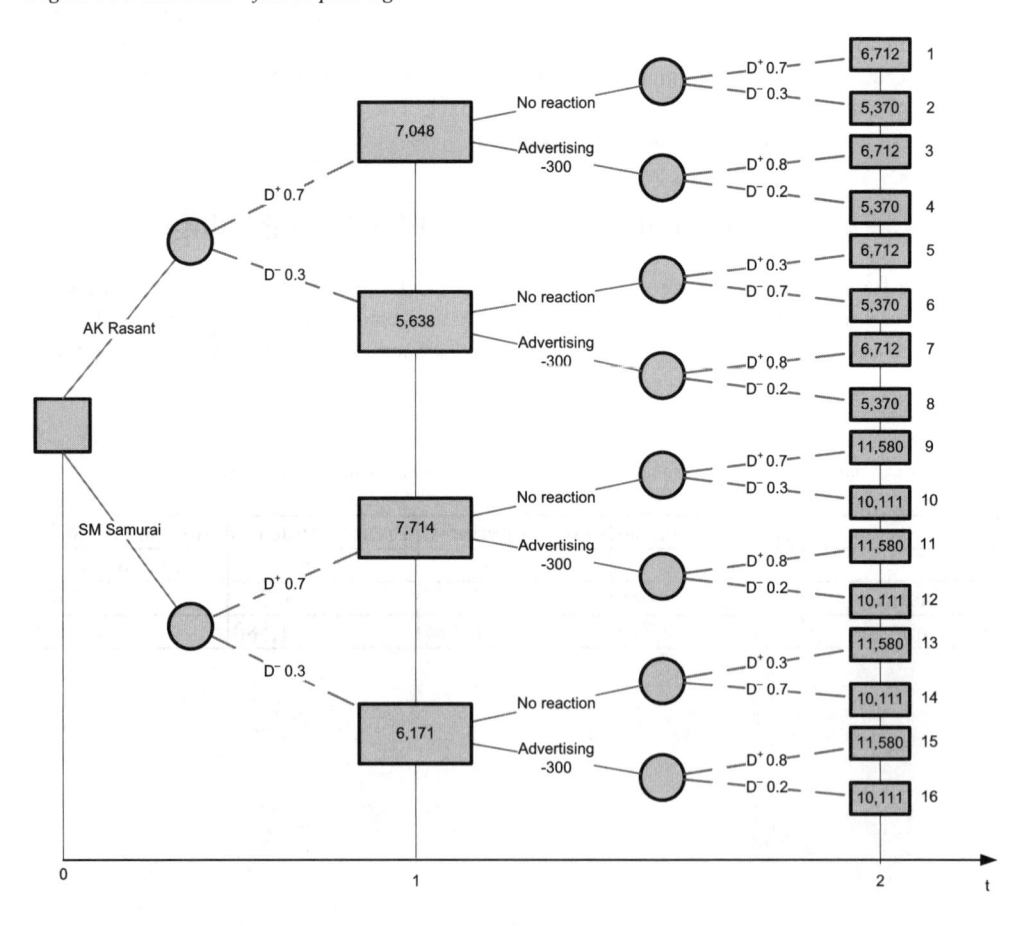

4.6 Decision Tree Analysis

We explain the decision tree from Figure 4-5. At the point of time t_0 a decision about the investment has to be made. Either the investor chooses alternative 1 (AK Rasant) or alternative 2 (SM Samurai). We look at the decision sequence following the choice of alternative 1. In period 1 we get the result from the investment, the expected cash flow. As with the fixed planning, we assume that the size of the cash flows depend on the state of the economy in period 1. Therefore, there is a probability node before the outcome of period 1. If the demand turns out to be favourable, then a cash flow of € 7,048 can be reached. If demand turns out to be unfavourable a cash flow of only € 5,638 can be reached.

The further description of the decision tree starts in period 1 in the upper node, that is we start with the assumption of having chosen alternative 1 in period 0 and that the demand turns out to be favourable in period 1. Now the investor can react to this situation and make a consequent decision. This is either continuing the investment project as it has been planned or the initiation of a marketing campaign to enhance the product's publicity. Again the expected result for the end of period 2 depends on the state of the economy in that period. As in period 1 the probability shows whether the economy turns out to be booming or to be in a recession. Table 4-20 shows the possible results for period 2:

Table 4-20 Explanation of the way to the results in period 2

Outcome in t_2	Action in t_1	State of the economy in period 2
Node 1	No reaction	Favourable
Node 2	No reaction	Unfavourable
Node 3	Advertising	Favourable
Node 4	Advertising	Unfavourable

These four possibilities occur if decision alternative 1 is chosen in t_0 and if the state of the economy turns out to be favourable. Thus, for the complete decision tree with two possibilities in t_0 and two possible states of the economies in t_1 for each alternative, there are 16 different outcomes. In Table 4-21 we compute the net present values for the final nodes in period 2.[24]

---

[24] The net present value in node 1 is exactly the same as the one which we derived for the AK Rasant using the net present value method with certainty. Here, this represents only one of eight possible outcomes in the final nodes for the AK Rasant. The values for SM Samurai cannot be compared to those of our earlier calculation, because now we refer to a time horizon of only two periods.

Table 4-21 Net present values in the final nodes in period 2 within the flexible planning approach

Outcome	Initial outlay	PV CF in period 1	PV CF in period 2	Advertising	NPV
Node 1	-9,000	7,048	6,712	0	4,760
Node 2	-9,000	7,048	5,370	0	3,418
Node 3	-9,000	7,048	6,712	-300	4,460
Node 4	-9,000	7,048	5,370	-300	3,118
Node 5	-9,000	5,638	6,712	0	3,350
Node 6	-9,000	5,638	5,370	0	2,008
Node 7	-9,000	5,638	6,712	-300	3,050
Node 8	-9,000	5,638	5,370	-300	1,708
Node 9	-14,000	7,714	11,580	0	5,294
Node 10	-14,000	7,714	10,111	0	3,825
Node 11	-14,000	7,714	11,580	-300	4,994
Node 12	-14,000	7,714	10,111	-300	3,525
Node 13	-14,000	6,171	11,580	0	3,751
Node 14	-14,000	6,171	10,111	0	2,282
Node 15	-14,000	6,171	11,580	-300	3,451
Node 16	-14,000	6,171	10,111	-300	1,982

The implementation of the flexible planning approach differs from the fixed planning approach in the fact that we start at the end of the time horizon with the results of the last period. Based on these results the expected net present values of all decision alternatives in each decision node are computed. The decision strategy that maximises the outcome is chosen and the worse alternatives are rejected successively. For further considerations only those alternatives are taken into account that maximise the expected net present values. These calculations must be continued until the beginning of planning period t_0 is reached and the optimal decision sequence is chosen.

In Table 4-22 we start the optimisation beginning in the final nodes. Thereto we identify the best decisions in t_1. In the point of time t_1 there are four outcome nodes, in which a decision has to be made either to launch the marketing campaign or to do nothing.

Table 4-22 Overview of the decision nodes in period 1

Decision node in t_1	Bought car	State of the economy
Situation 1	AK Rasant	positive
Situation 2	AK Rasant	negative
Situation 3	SM Samurai	positive
Situation 4	SM Samurai	negative

4.6 Decision Tree Analysis

In Tables 4-23 and 4-24 we calculate the expected net present values in the decision nodes under consideration of the probabilities for high respective low demand. As an example we compute the expected net present values for the first decision node in t_1.

Table 4-23 Calculation of the expected net present value for the action 'no reaction'

Action: No reaction			
Node	NPV	Probability	Weighted net present value
1	4,760	0.7	3,332
2	3,418	0.3	1,025
Expected net present value			4,357

Table 4-24 Calculation of the expected net present value for the action 'advertising'

Action: Advertising			
Node	NPV	Probability	Weighted net present value
3	4,460	0.8	3,568
4	3,118	0.2	624
Expected net present value			4,192

The expected net present values in the other nodes are calculated in the same way.

Table 4-25 Summary of the expected net present values for the decision nodes in period 1

Decision node in t_1	State of the economy	Expected net preset value while 'no reaction'	Expected net preset value while 'advertising'
Situation 1	positive	€ 4,357	€ 4,192
Situation 2	negative	€ 2,411	€ 2,782
Situation 3	positive	€ 4,853	€ 4,700
Situation 4	negative	€ 2,723	€ 3,157

If a decision based on the expected net present values from Table 4-25 were made, then the decisions in Table 4-26 would be useful:

Table 4-26 Summary of useful decisions in the decision nodes of period 1

Decision node in t_1	Action	Net present value
Situation 1	No reaction	€ 4,357
Situation 2	Advertising	€ 2,782
Situation 3	No reaction	€ 4,853
Situation 4	Advertising	€ 3,157

Now we move back for one more period and consider only the best consecutive decisions for the alternatives in period t_0:

AK Rasant: € 4,357 × 0.7 + € 2,782 × 0.3 = € 3,885

SM Samurai: € 4,853 × 0.7 + € 3,157 × 0.3 = € 4,344

According to this calculation the SM Samurai would still be preferable. The optimum consecutive decision is the following: If demand turns out to be booming in period 1, then the project should be continued as planned. If, however, demand turns out to be negative in period 1, then a marketing campaign should be launched.

4.6.4 Evaluation of the Decision Tree Analysis

1. The decision tree analysis allows structuring complex investment decisions because the decision alternatives are presented precisely. It gives a clear picture of the possible consequences of the decisions faced by the company's management.

2. The action of deciding becomes comprehensible. Changes in planning and the consideration of consecutive decisions are possible.

3. The decision tree allows the state of the economy to change on a year-by-year basis.

4. A decision tree usually is time consuming to construct, depending on the complexity of the situation.

5. The quantification of input data is difficult, especially the estimate of probabilities.

6. The amelioration of the technique from fixed planning to flexible planning covers all kind of possible activities for the investor and possibly leads to clearer decisions but demands considerably more effort for the planning. If for the state of the economy not only the states 'good' and 'bad', but also values in between are accepted and in addition to further determining factors for the economic situation, then the decision tree very quickly becomes illegible.

7. The assessment of investments using expected values is based on the assumption of risk neutral investors. Probability distributions for net present values can be included but that further lowers the practical applicability. However, appropriate computer programs are available.

8. As with all other techniques of investment appraisal, finally the investor is faced with a useful trade-off between planning accuracy on one side and practicability on the other.

4.7 Summary and Evaluation

Under the conditions of certainty we have been considering a situation where there is one clear possible outcome. While applying the non-discounting investment appraisal methods these are costs, profit, accounting rate of return or the payback period. Within the application of the discounting models of investment appraisal these are the net present value, the annuity and the internal rate of return or the discounting payback period. Usually the approaches available under the conditions of risk take as their starting point the net present value method.

If the applied input variables are uncertain, then the investment appraisal techniques discussed in this chapter provide us with some indication as to what the right answer with regard to managerial decision making might look like. The easiest but most inexact way is the correction method. Somehow more extensive is the sensitivity analysis, which has the advantage of describing a band width of the calculated outcome or critical values. Risk analysis provides a frequency distribution and as a result a risk profile of the net present value. Setting up a decision tree provides assessment of multi-sequential investment alternatives under consideration of occurrence probabilities. So, even in absence of certainty, the application of investment appraisal techniques is still valid.

4.8 Exercises with Answers

4.8.1 Exercises

Exercise 4-1 Investment decision making under uncertainty – Correction method

The management of a university plans to ameliorate the conditions of studying in a certain degree course. To reach this aim there are two basic different possibilities:

1. Construction of a computer workroom which will be exclusively used by this group of students.
2. Assignment of personnel to address themselves to the concerns of this group of students.

For both possibilities it is assumed that more students can be attracted so that the university can make a profit from higher tuition fees by € 14,400 per year. The financial details for the computer workroom are as follows: Initial outlay: € 100,000, estimated economic life: 10 years, annual maintenance costs: € 2,000. The annual personnel costs for administration staff would be € 12,000. To evaluate investment projects the university uses a discount rate of 6 %.

a) Which of the two possibilities do you prefer according to the net present value method? Assume that the initial outlay for the computer workroom is paid in two instalments at the beginning and at the end of the first year of use. For convenience we assume that all other payments – if relevant – occur in a single sum at the end of the year.

b) Apply the correction method while assuming that the increase in tuition fees is only € 10,000 per year. How would your conclusions differ from the answer in subtask a?

c) How would your results differ from subtask b, if you in addition to that cut the discount rate from 6 % to 3 %?

Exercise 4-2 Investment decision making under uncertainty – Sensitivity analysis

The municipal administration is responsible for the maintenance of school buildings. In a storage room, a kitchen is to be installed in order to offer the pupils a warm meal. The equipment would cost € 10,000. The necessary installations for electricity and water plus the ventilation system cost an additional € 2,000. For the entire equipment, a useful life expectancy of 10 years is assumed. The municipality has to carry the cleaning cost of € 500 per year.

The investment aims at generating income through renting the cafeteria. The city council requires a rate of return for capital invested of 3 %. According to the lease contract the leaseholder bears all other operating costs, including maintenance. The rent should be 0.5 % of the revenues. Monthly revenues of € 40,000 are estimated.

a) What is the project's accounting rate of return? Make appropriate recommendations to assist the city council in decision making.

b) Conduct a sensitivity analysis on the variable sales revenues: How sensitive is your result from subtask a if you recalculate the accounting rate of return for levels of monthly sales revenues of € 30,000 or € 50,000?

c) What is the net present value under the different assumptions about the sales revenues of the locater? Assume that all cash flows are paid year-end.

4.8 Exercises with Answers

Exercise 4-3 Investment decision making under uncertainty – Risk analysis

A leisure park's management intends to buy a little train, which provides the visitors of the parks with the possibility to take round trips. The estimated investment costs are € 630,000 for the little train and another € 1.5 Mio. for the restoration of already existing rails on which the train should run. For all equipment the economic life is estimated as 20 years after having started the business.

The management has gathered the following information:

- At the beginning of year 1 they have to pay a planning cost of € 80,000 for engineering consultants.
- The payments for the rails occur one half each at the beginning of the first year and at the end of the first year.
- The train is paid for at the beginning of the first year and immediately put into operation. Consequently, there are assumed no time delays throughout construction.
- Current maintenance costs occur at the end of the respective period at the annual amount of € 5,000.
- With the purchase of the railway the management expects the number of visitors to rise by 200 people daily each paying a fare of € 3.00. We assume that these cash inflows of a year occur as a whole at the end of the respective year.
- A discount rate of 4 % is judged appropriate.

a) Compute the net present value of the investment project under certainty.

b) Now, run a risk analysis under the following conditions:

- 1) Selection of the uncertain input variables

  We assume that the cash inflow is uncertain. They can be 30 % under, but also 30 % above the value under certainty. Accordingly the following figures for the cash inflow are possible: € 153,300, € 219,000 or € 284,700.

- 2) Estimate of the probability distributions of the uncertain input variables

Table 4-27 Probability distributions of the uncertain input variable

Sales revenues in €	153,300	219,000	284,700
Probability	0.4	0.5	0.1

- 3) Allocation and generation of random numbers for the uncertain input variables

Table 4-28 Allocation of random numbers to the uncertain input variable

Sales revenues in €	153,300	219,000	284,700
Allocated random numbers	1, 2, 3, 4	5, 6, 7, 8, 9	10

Table 4-29 Generated random numbers for the uncertain input variable 'sales revenues'

Replicate	1	2	3	4	5	6	7	8
Random numbers for the revenues	6	3	9	1	2	10	9	3

Now calculate the related net present values. Prepare calculations for the relative frequencies of the net present value and derive a risk profile. Make appropriate investment recommendations.

Exercise 4-4 Investment decision making under uncertainty – Decision tree analysis: flexible planning

Close to a castle, possibly nominated for the list of the UNESCO World Heritage, an investor wants to build a leisure park. The listing would significantly increase the name recognition of the castle and therefore bring so many users into the leisure park as to assure its success. The investor has to decide to either build a huge park immediately or to wait until he could be sure of the development of demand. In this case, he would build only a small park with the option to expand after the first period. The immediate investment into a large-scale park is less expensive but also more risky than the split into two smaller investments. In case of an extension of the small investment in period 2, paybacks of the same amount as with a large-scale investment are possible.

We look at a time horizon of two periods. The appropriate discount rate is 10 %. These are the cash outflows of the investment in MU, whereas the sum for the enlargement of the small facility in t_1 is the already discounted value to period t_0:

4.8 Exercises with Answers

	Point in time t_0	Point in time t_1
Large facility	-140	0
Small facility	-80	0
Enlargement of the small facility	0	-80

The cash flows in each period depend on the development of the state of the economy. The following probabilities of occurrence are estimated for the state of the economy:

Period 1	$p(h_1) = 0.9; p(l_1) = 0.1$
Period 2	$p(h_2/h_1) = 0.9; p(l_2/h_1) = 0.1$
	$p(h_2/l_1) = 0.1; p(l_2/l_1) = 0.9$

The estimated cash flows in each period will be as follows:

	Present value cash flow in period 1		Present value cash flow in period 2	
	High demand	Low demand	High demand	Low demand
Small facility	50	30	50	30
Large facility	80	30	80	30

a) Diagram a decision tree to structure the decision management is facing.

b) Calculate the net present values for the outcome nodes in period 2.

c) State clearly whether the investor should start small and if appropriate enlarge the facility after period 1 or whether it is more attractive to start right away with a large facility.

4.8.2 Answers

Answer to exercise 4-1 Investment decision making under uncertainty – Correction method

a) Computer workroom

Point in time	PVF	Cash inflows	Cash outflows	Cash flows	PV Cash flows
0	1.0000	14,400.00	52,000.00	-37,600.00	-37,600.00
1	0.9434	14,400.00	52,000.00	-37,600.00	-35,471.84
2	0.8900	14,400.00	2,000.00	12,400.00	11,036.00
3	0.8396	14,400.00	2,000.00	12,400.00	10,411.04
4	0.7921	14,400.00	2,000.00	12,400.00	9,822.04
5	0.7473	14,400.00	2,000.00	12,400.00	9,266.52
6	0.7050	14,400.00	2,000.00	12,400.00	8,742.00
7	0.6651	14,400.00	2,000.00	12,400.00	8,247.24
8	0.6274	14,400.00	2,000.00	12,400.00	7,779.76
9	0.5919	14,400.00	2,000.00	12,400.00	7,339.56
10	0.5584	0.00	0.00	0.00	0.00
NPV					-427.68

Personnel

Point in time	PVF	Cash inflows	Cash outflows	Cash flows	PV Cash flows
0	1.0000	14,400.00	12,000.00	2,400.00	2,400.00
1	0.9434	14,400.00	12,000.00	2,400.00	2,264.16
2	0.8900	14,400.00	12,000.00	2,400.00	2,136.00
3	0.8396	14,400.00	12,000.00	2,400.00	2,015.04
4	0.7921	14,400.00	12,000.00	2,400.00	1,901.04
5	0.7473	14,400.00	12,000.00	2,400.00	1,793.52
6	0.7050	14,400.00	12,000.00	2,400.00	1,692.00
7	0.6651	14,400.00	12,000.00	2,400.00	1,596.24
8	0.6274	14,400.00	12,000.00	2,400.00	1,505.76
9	0.5919	14,400.00	12,000.00	2,400.00	1,420.56
10	0.5584	0.00	0.00	0.00	0.00
NPV					18,724.32

According to this the alternative personnel would be preferable.

4.8 Exercises with Answers

b) Computer workroom

Point in time	PVF	Cash inflows	Cash outflows	Cash flows	PV Cash flows
0	1.0000	10,000.00	52,000.00	-42,000.00	-42,000.00
1	0.9434	10,000.00	52,000.00	-42,000.00	-39,622,80
2	0.8900	10,000.00	2,000.00	8,000.00	7,120.00
3	0.8396	10,000.00	2,000.00	8,000.00	6,716.80
4	0.7921	10,000.00	2,000.00	8,000.00	6,336.80
5	0.7473	10,000.00	2,000.00	8,000.00	5,978.40
6	0.7050	10,000.00	2,000.00	8,000.00	5,640.00
7	0.6651	10,000.00	2,000.00	8,000.00	5,320.80
8	0.6274	10,000.00	2,000.00	8,000.00	5,019.20
9	0.5919	10,000.00	2,000.00	8,000.00	4,735.20
10	0.5584	0.00	0.00	0.00	0.00
NPV					-34,755.60

Personnel

Point in time	PVF	Cash inflows	Cash outflows	Cash flows	PV Cash flows
0	1.0000	10,000.00	12,000.00	-2,000.00	-2,000.00
1	0.9434	10,000.00	12,000.00	-2,000.00	-1,886.80
2	0.8900	10,000.00	12,000.00	-2,000.00	-1,780.00
3	0.8396	10,000.00	12,000.00	-2,000.00	-1,679.20
4	0.7921	10,000.00	12,000.00	-2,000.00	-1,584.20
5	0.7473	10,000.00	12,000.00	-2,000.00	-1,494.60
6	0.7050	10,000.00	12,000.00	-2,000.00	-1,410.00
7	0.6651	10,000.00	12,000.00	-2,000.00	-1,330.20
8	0.6274	10,000.00	12,000.00	-2,000.00	-1,254.80
9	0.5919	10,000.00	12,000.00	-2,000.00	-1,183.80
10	0.5584	0.00	0.00	0.00	0.00
NPV					-15,603.60

Under the new conditions neither of the alternatives is preferable.

c) Computer workroom

Point in time	PVF	Cash inflows	Cash outflows	Cash flows	PV Cash flows
0	1.0000	10,000.00	52,000.00	-42,000.00	-42,000.00
1	0.9709	10,000.00	52,000.00	-42,000.00	-40,777.80
2	0.9426	10,000.00	2,000.00	8,000.00	7,540.80
3	0.9151	10,000.00	2,000.00	8,000.00	7,320.80
4	0.8885	10,000.00	2,000.00	8,000.00	7,108.00
5	0.8626	10,000.00	2,000.00	8,000.00	6,900.80
6	0.8375	10,000.00	2,000.00	8,000.00	6,700.00
7	0.8131	10,000.00	2,000.00	8,000.00	6,504.80
8	0.7894	10,000.00	2,000.00	8,000.00	6,315.20
9	0.7664	10,000.00	2,000.00	8,000.00	6,131.20
10	0.7441	0.00	0.00	0.00	0.00
NPV					-28,256.20

Personnel

Point in time	PVF	Cash inflows	Cash outflows	Cash flows	PV Cash flows
0	1.0000	10,000.00	12,000.00	-2,000.00	-2,000.00
1	0.9709	10,000.00	12,000.00	-2,000.00	-1,941.80
2	0.9426	10,000.00	12,000.00	-2,000.00	-1,885.20
3	0.9151	10,000.00	12,000.00	-2,000.00	-1,830.20
4	0.8885	10,000.00	12,000.00	-2,000.00	-1,777.00
5	0.8626	10,000.00	12,000.00	-2,000.00	-1,725.20
6	0.8375	10,000.00	12,000.00	-2,000.00	-1,675.00
7	0.8131	10,000.00	12,000.00	-2,000.00	-1,626.20
8	0.7894	10,000.00	12,000.00	-2,000.00	-1,578.80
9	0.7664	10,000.00	12,000.00	-2,000.00	-1,532.80
10	0.7441	0.00	0.00	0.00	0.00
NPV					-17,572.20

Therefore, there is still no preferable alternative.

Answer to exercise 4-2 Investment decision making under uncertainty – Sensitivity analysis

a)

$$\text{Accounting rate of return} = \frac{\text{Average annual profit}}{\text{Average capital employed}} \times 100$$

Equipment in the kitchen € 10,000
+ Costs for installation   € 2,000
Total costs   € 12,000

4.8 Exercises with Answers

With an anticipated economic life of 10 years, we get the following annual depreciation rates: € 12,000 ÷ 10 years = € 1,200.

Rent: € 40,000 per month. € 40,000 × 12 = € 480,000 annual rent.
Thereof 0.5 %: € 480,000 × 0.005 = € 2,400.

The average annual profit is calculated as follows:

Revenues	€ 2,400
− Depreciation	€ 1,200
− Cleaning	€ 500
= Profit	€ 700

$$\text{Average annual capital employed} = \frac{\text{Initial outlay}}{2} = \frac{€12{,}000}{2} = €6{,}000$$

So the accounting rate of return is: $\frac{€700}{€6{,}000} \times 100 = 11.7\%$

Thus, the project is desirable.

b)

1. Sales revenues € 30,000 per month

The average annual profit is calculated as follows:

Revenues	1.800 €
− Depreciation	1.200 €
− Cleaning	500 €
= Profit	100 €

So the accounting rate of return is: $\frac{€100}{€6{,}000} \times 100 = 1.7\%$

Thus, the investment is no longer worthwhile.

2. Sales revenues € 50,000 per month

The average annual profit is calculated as follows

Revenues	€ 3,000
− Depreciation	€ 1,200
− Cleaning	€ 500
= Profit	€ 1,300

So the accounting rate of return is: $\frac{€1{,}300}{€6{,}000} \times 100 = 21.7\%$

Hence, the investment is desirable. In comparison with subtask a the accounting rate of return increased by a considerable amount.

c)

Sales revenues per month	Annual rent	Annual cleaning	Cash flow non-discounted values
€ 30,000	€ 1,800	€ 500	€ 1,300
€ 40,000	€ 2,400	€ 500	€ 1,900
€ 50,000	€ 3,000	€ 500	€ 2,500

Multiplying the present values of the cash flows by the PVA yields:

Alternative 1: PVA (10 years, 3 %) 8.5302 × € 1,300 = € 11,089
Alternative 2: PVA (10 years, 3 %) 8.5302 × € 1,900 = € 16,207
Alternative 3: PVA (10 years, 3 %) 8.5302 × € 2,500 = € 21,326

By subtracting the initial outlay we get the following net present values:

Alternative 1: € 11,089 – € 12,000 = € –911
Alternative 2: € 16,207 – € 12,000 = € 4,207
Alternative 3: € 21,326 – € 12,000 = € 9,326

The result shows that the net present value turns negative for the worse alternative 1. In this case the investment would not be worth pursuing.

Answer to exercise 4-3 Investment decision making under uncertainty – Risk analysis

a)

Payments occurring	PVF or PVA	Advice	Current value	Present value
Planning	1	Beginning year 1	-80,000	-80,000
Rails	1	50 %: Beginning year 1	-750,000	-750,000
Rails	0.9615	50 %: End year 1	-750,000	-721,125
Little train	1	Beginning year 1	-630,000	-630,000
Maintenance	13.5903	PVA 4 %, 20 years	-5,000	-67,952
Subtotal				-2,249,077
Cash inflow fares	13.5903	PVA 4 %, 20 years	219,000	2,976,276
Net present values				727,199

Under conditions of certainty the net present value is € 727,199. It is above zero, and the investment project appears profitable.

4.8 Exercises with Answers

b)

- Step 4 of the risk analysis: Calculation of the net present values

Replicate	Current value of cash inflow	PVA	Present value of cash inflow	Discounted cash outflow	Net present value
1	219,000	13.5903	2,976,276	-2,249,077	727,199
2	153,300	13.5903	2,083,393	-2,249,077	-165,684
3	219,000	13.5903	2,976,276	-2,249,077	727,199
4	153,300	13.5903	2,083,393	-2,249,077	-165,684
5	153,300	13.5903	2,083,393	-2,249,077	-165,684
6	284,700	13.5903	3,869,158	-2,249,077	1,620,081
7	219,000	13.5903	2,976,276	-2,249,077	727,199
8	153,300	13.5903	2,083,393	-2,249,077	-165,684

- Step 5 of the risk analysis: Calculation of the relative frequencies of the net present value and derivation of the risk profile

Net present value	Relative frequency	Cumulative relative frequency
1,620,081	0.125	0.125
727,199	0.375	0.500
-165,684	0.500	1.000

The computed net present values are used to plot the following risk profile

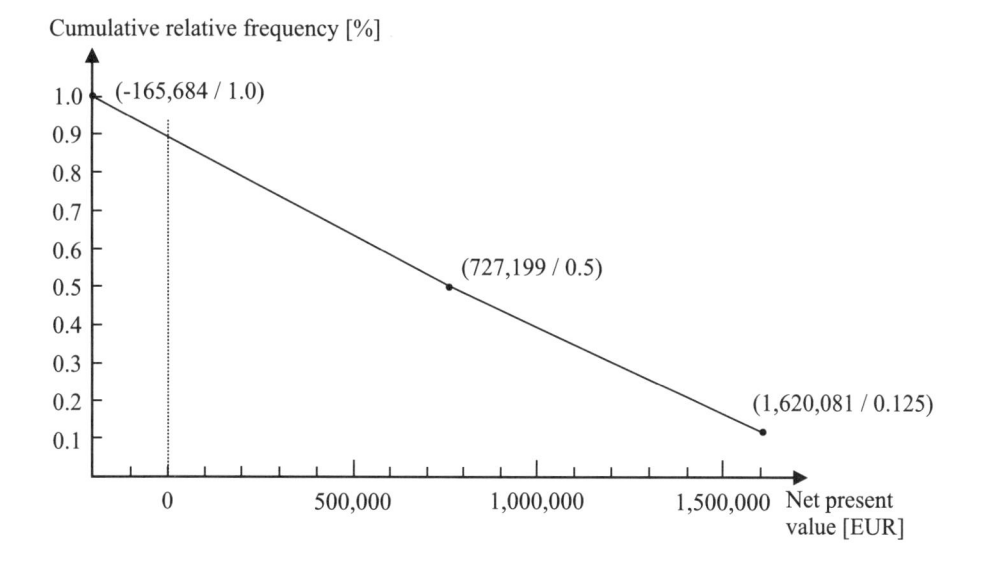

Cumulative relative frequency [%]

(-165,684 / 1.0)

(727,199 / 0.5)

(1,620,081 / 0.125)

Net present value [EUR]

146   4 Investment Decision Making under Conditions of Uncertainty

- Step 6 of the risk analysis: Interpretation of the results

    We see that the net present value is positive only with a probability of 50 %. However, in another 50 % we have to expect negative net present values.

Answer to exercise 4-4 Investment decision making under uncertainty – Decision tree analysis: flexible planning

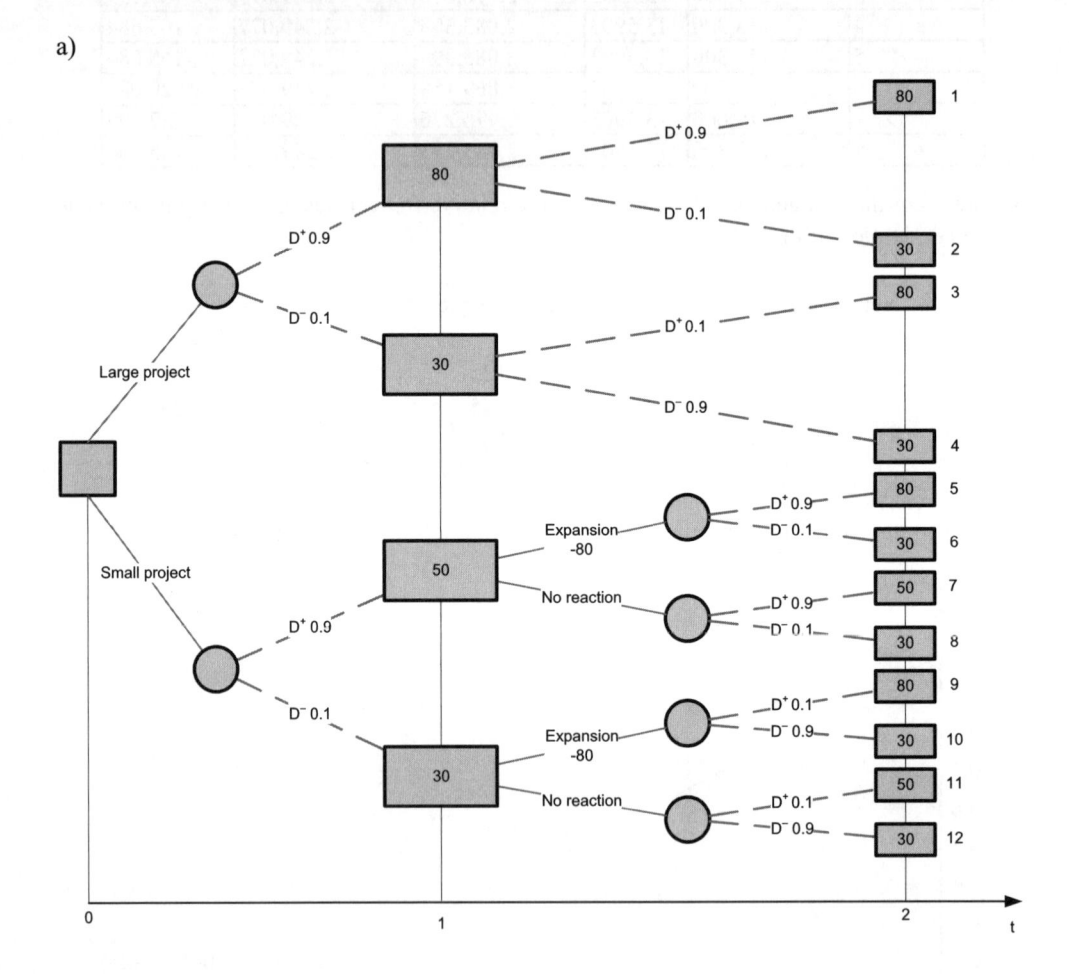

a)

[Decision tree diagram]

Large project branch (D^+ 0.9 / D^- 0.1):
- Period 1: 80 → D^+ 0.9 → 80 (outcome 1); D^- 0.1 → 30 (outcome 2)
- Period 1: 30 → D^+ 0.1 → 80 (outcome 3); D^- 0.9 → 30 (outcome 4)

Small project branch (D^+ 0.9 / D^- 0.1):
- Period 1: 50 → Expansion -80 → D^+ 0.9 → 80 (5); D^- 0.1 → 30 (6)
- Period 1: 50 → No reaction → D^+ 0.9 → 50 (7); D^- 0.1 → 30 (8)
- Period 1: 30 → Expansion -80 → D^+ 0.1 → 80 (9); D^- 0.9 → 30 (10)
- Period 1: 30 → No reaction → D^+ 0.1 → 50 (11); D^- 0.9 → 30 (12)

Time axis: 0, 1, 2, t

b)

We started with the present values of the cash flows in periods 1 and 2. Thus, to derive the net present values, we can move forward with these values without any transformation. These are the net present values in the outcome nodes of period 2:

4.8 Exercises with Answers

Outcome	Initial outlay	PV CF in period 1	PV CF in period 2	Expansion	Net present value
Node 1	-140	80	80	0	20
Node 2	-140	80	30	0	-30
Node 3	-140	30	80	0	-30
Node 4	-140	30	30	0	-80
Node 5	-80	50	80	-80	-30
Node 6	-80	50	30	-80	-80
Node 7	-80	50	50	0	20
Node 8	-80	50	30	0	0
Node 9	-80	30	80	-80	-50
Node 10	-80	30	30	-80	-100
Node 11	-80	30	50	0	0
Node 12	-80	30	30	0	-20

Now we calculate the expected net present values in the decision nodes taking into account the probability of occurrence for a high or a low demand.

Action: None			
Node	NPV	Probability	Weighted net present value
1	20	0.9	18
2	-30	0.1	-3
Expected net present value			15

Action: None			
Node	NPV	Probability	Weighted net present value
3	-30	0.1	-3
4	-80	0.9	-72
Expected net present value			-75

Action: Enlargement of the small facility			
Node	NPV	Probability	Weighted net present value
5	-30	0.9	-27
6	-80	0.1	-8
Expected net present value			-35

Action: None			
Node	NPV	Probability	Weighted net present value
7	20	0.9	18
8	0	0.1	0
Expected net present value			18

Action: Enlargement of the small facility			
Node	NPV	Probability	Weighted net present value
9	-50	0.1	-5
10	-100	0.9	-90
Expected net present value			-95

Action: None			
Node	NPV	Probability	Weighted net present value
11	0	0.1	0
12	-20	0.9	-18
Expected net present value			-18

We summarise the results:

Decision node in t_1	State of the economy	Expected net present value in case of 'no reaction'	Expected net present value in case of expanding the small facility
Situation 1	positive	15 MU	–
Situation 2	negative	– 75 MU	–
Situation 3	positive	18 MU	– 35 MU
Situation 4	negative	– 18 MU	– 95 MU

Now if based on the expected net present values, a decision is made, then the following decisions are desirable:

Decision node in t_1	Action	Expected net present value
Situation 1	No reaction	15 MU
Situation 2	No reaction	– 75 MU
Situation 3	No reaction	18 MU
Situation 4	No reaction	– 18 MU

Now we move back for one more period and consider for the alternatives only the best consecutive decisions in period t_0:

Large facility: 15 MU × 0.9 + (–75 MU) × 0.1 = 6 MU
Small facility: 18 MU × 0.9 + (–18 MU) × 0.1 = 14.4 MU

As a result of this calculation it is worthwhile starting small in t_0. Regardless whether demand turns out to be positive or negative afterwards, it is never useful to expand the small facility.

5 Advanced Topics of Investment Appraisal

5.1 Learning Objectives

In Chapter 4 we have already started to relax the simplifying assumptions made with regard to the net present value's calculation which we used in the three previous chapters. After studying Chapter 4 the decision maker knows how to assess an investment project under the conditions of risk and uncertainty. In this chapter we move forward: Step by step we are going to introduce additional aspects to derive more advanced solutions. This chapter sets out

- that we need to give attention to the problems which arise for the investment appraisal process by the existence of taxation.
- We learn how to adapt the investment appraisal techniques to inflation.
- We separate the investment decision from the financing decision and learn how the influence of financing can be addressed by setting up a 'complete financial plan'.
- Utility analyses allow us to consider subjective and non-monetary influences on the investment decision.
- Finally, for decision-makers within the public sector you will get acquainted with cost-benefit-analyses which belong to the macroeconomic methods of investment appraisal.
- As in the previous chapters you will find the advantages and disadvantages of each method at the end of each advanced topic of investment appraisal.
- A Summary and evaluation as well as worked examples will finish this last chapter as the chapters before.

At this stage it is worth pointing out that we return to the assumption of certainty. By so doing we can focus on the new issues under discussion.

5.2 Taxation

5.2.1 Introduction

So far, we have based our analysis on the assumption that all cash inflow and cash outflow from an investment had been adjusted for tax implications. Now, taxes are introduced explicitly. An investment project can be completely appraised only if full consideration is given to all taxation implications. Tax payments caused by the investment must be estimated and integrated into the derivation of the net present value. To calculate the net present value we have been considering the following equation:

Net present value = Present value of cash inflow – Present value of cash outflow

These are the input variables to derive the net present value:

- the employed discount rate,
- the estimated cash inflow, including possible salvage values,
- the estimated cash outflow and
- the anticipated average life.

We have to examine which of these input variables will change considering taxation. Cost taxes like motor vehicle taxes or property acquisition taxes are regarded as normal cash outflow of the investment and are therefore directly considered within the investment's estimated cash flow. When a used asset is sold we assume that it is sold at its book-value, the remaining basis for depreciable assets. Then there will be no loss or gain on the sale und thus no tax consequences.[25] However, taxes on income must be considered in another way. Taxes on profits are, for example, income taxes and church taxes[26] of the shareholders, trade earnings tax for individual enterprises or business partnerships as well as corporate income tax and trade earnings tax for corporations.

Taxes have to be paid on the reported income of the company. In order to follow the impact of taxation on investments it is necessary to trace the implications of taxes over the life of an investment. The calculation of an investment's net present value is based on the present values of cash inflow and cash outflow. However, taxes are not based on cash flows, but on taxable income. Therefore, an auxiliary calculation is necessary to show the connection between the cash flow of the investment and the respective taxable profit.

---

[25] For taxes on the sale of an existing asset cf. Wöhe, Günter, Einführung in die Allgemeine Betriebswirtschaftslehre, op. cit., pp. 619-620.

[26] Church taxes conform to the level of the income tax.

5.2 Taxation

It is beyond the scope of this book to examine the German or any other country's particular tax system and its implications on investment appraisal techniques.[27] Tax laws vary not only among different countries but also over time within a single country. As a consequence the tax regime impacts upon project appraisal discussed here concentrate on main principles which could be used reasonably for various real tax systems. In no way does our analysis represent the real world of taxation, but it allows conclusions that do have real-world validity. With this in mind, we make the following assumptions:[28]

- The profits of a company are subject to a general tax rate which is independent from the legal structure of the company. This must be imagined as a condensed tax rate for all kinds of profits.
- This flat tax rate on profits is: 0 < tax rate < 1. The tax on profits operates as proportional tax with a constant marginal tax rate. A rate of profit tax 0.4 respective 40 % means that on each unit of incremental profit 0.4 units of tax has to be paid.[29]
- Tax payable is a cash outflow; tax receivable is a cash inflow at the end of each period.[30]
- Profit is defined as the company's revenues minus allowable costs. The initial outlay can be set against taxable profits through the depreciation rate since the first period of the investment's life. For convenience we assume that accounting depreciation and tax-allowable depreciation are the same.
- The expense of interest on debt is completely tax-deductible.

Taxation implications on investment decision have two diametrical effects:

- The consideration of taxation leads to a correction of the input variable 'cash flow'. The investment's cash flow has to be reduced by the level of tax to be paid. Thus, the net present value drops in comparison with the net present value before taxes.
- Similarly the discount rate changes. If the investment is financed with equity, then the net profit for the best opportunity changes through the tax burden. If the interest on the best opportunity is i.e. 5 % before taxes and if the company is taxed at the rate of 40 %, then, due to the taxation, the interest rate falls to 3 %. Financing the investment with debt capital also leads to lower discount rates, because interest on debt is often tax-deductible. With a general tax rate of 40 % the cost of capital drops from 5 % to 3 %.[31] Thus, the discount rate falls in any case independently of the way the investment is financed. If the

---

[27] For a survey about principal German taxes and their consideration in investment appraisal cf. Kruschwitz, Lutz, Investitionsrechnung, op. cit., pp. 118-128.

[28] Cf. also Wöhe, Günter, Einführung in die Allgemeine Betriebswirtschaftslehre, op. cit., pp. 616-620.

[29] This may vary from the progressive tax tariffs in German tax law. But this is done for a better understanding of these problems.

[30] Tax refunds may occur if losses at the beginning of an investment lower the tax basis for the whole company. In these cases the tax refund can be partly attributed to the investment project.

[31] $0.05 \times (1 - 0.4) = 0.03$.

discount rate goes down, the net present value will go up compared to the net present value without taxes.

Usually one can expect that the first effect is greater than the second one and that the net present value after taxes is lower than the net present value before taxes. But if the effect on interest rates surmounts the drop of the cash flows, then the net present value can rise and an investment project, which had a negative net present value before taxes and which was therefore rejected, can turn out to be acceptable. In this case we observe what is called the paradox of taxation.

We summarise our results in Table 5-1. If we compute the net present value without taxes, then we discount the cash flows with the respective discount rate. We calculate the net present value after taxes by subtracting the taxable income multiplied by the tax rate from the cash flow. Then this result is discounted by the factor (1–tax rate) which is a reduced discount rate.

Table 5-1: Calculation of the net present value without and with taxes

Net present value without taxes	Net present value with taxes
$NPV = \sum_{t=1}^{n} CF_t \times (1+i)^{-t}$	$NPV = \sum_{t=1}^{n} \frac{[CF_t - \text{tax rate} \times (CF_t - \text{Depreciation}_t)]}{[1+i \times (1-\text{tax rate})]^t}$

5.2.2 Comparison of Alternatives

The basic principles in determining cash flow after tax are outlined below in Table 5-2 by presenting the appropriate format for their calculation.

Table 5-2 Derivation of the project's after tax cash flow

Vehicle	AK Rasant	SM Samurai
Project cash flow before tax	7,400	8,100
- Depreciation	4,500	4,667
= Taxable income	2,900	3,433
- Tax payable	1,160	1,373
= Income after tax	1,740	2,060
+ Depreciation	4,500	4,667
= After tax cash flow	6,240	6,727

5.2 Taxation

To derive the net present value without taxes we used the following data (Table 5-3):

Table 5-3 Basic data for the calculation of the net present values without taxes

	AK Rasant	SM Samurai
Initial outlay	9,000	14,000
Present value of an annuity	1.8594	2.7232
Cash flow per period	7,400	8,100
Net present value	4,760	8,058
Difference between net present values		3,298

With a discount rate of 5 % the net present value of the SM Samurai equals € 8,058 and, therefore, it exceeds the net present value of the AK Rasant by € 3,298 €.

In Table 5-4 we recalculate the net present value based on the corrected cash flow.

Table 5-4 Calculation of net present values after tax

	AK Rasant	SM Samurai
Initial outlay	9,000	14,000
Present value of an annuity	1.8594	2.7232
Cash flow per period	6,240	6,727
Net present value	2,603	4,319
Difference between net present values		1,716

The net present value of the SM Samurai falls to € 4,319. But it still exceeds that of the AK Rasant. To calculate this value, we still used the initial discount rate of 5 %. To show that the net present value rises by the corrected discount rate we recalculate Table 5-5 with the changed present value annuity factor. Here, we assume that corporation profit tax is charged at 40 %. The discount rate after tax, therefore, falls from 5 % to 3 %.

Table 5-5 Comparison of alternatives based on net present values after tax

	AK Rasant	SM Samurai
Initial outlay	9,000	14,000
Present value of an annuity	1.9135	2.8286
Cash flow per period	6,240	6,727
Net present value	2,940	5,028
Difference between net presen values		2,088

Still the SM Samurai would be preferable. Now, the net present value rises to € 5,028, but it is overall lower than the net present value before tax which was € 8,058. The net present value remains positive and hence the whole investment project is still profitable.

5.2.3 Evaluation of Taxation

1. A tax liability will arise on taxable profit of the whole company. To calculate the tax regime impacts upon a single investment on taxable income, we made simplifying assumptions.

2. First, the after-tax project cash flows have to be calculated. Then the discount rate employed in project analysis has to be adjusted to an after-tax rate.

3. Depreciation is considered within net present value evaluations only because of its tax effects. Depreciation is a process of recognising that assets wear out over time, but they are not cash outflow.

4. Comparing the net present values with and without taxes shows the influence of the tax relief through depreciation allowance.

5. Due to the simplifying assumptions the actual tax burden on profits is expected to be no more than an approximation.

6. The decision maker needs a good understanding of the tax system under which the company is liable to pay tax.

5.3 Inflation

5.3.1 Introduction

So far, we have assumed in our analysis that there are no general price movements within the economy. In reality, as all economies are characterised by changes in the purchasing power of money, we have to check whether price changes, either upwards (inflation) or downwards (deflation), are relevant to investment decisions. We must identify the influence that inflation has on the cash flows of an investment project and adapt the investment appraisal techniques if needed.

General price movements changing the level of consumption will influence the investment appraisal in two ways. On one side it makes the estimate of the project's cash flow more difficult. On the other side market interest rates can be expected to rise in case of general inflation. Thus, the investment appraisal must recognise expected inflation in the future cash flows and in addition, use a discount rate reflecting the investors' expectations about future inflation.

5.3 Inflation

The importance of inflation can easily be shown by an example considering a situation in which there is zero inflation. An investor is willing to invest € 100 in a project provided he receives € 110 in one year's time. Hence, the investor's discount rate or required rate of return is 10 % (€ 100 × 1.1 = € 110). Now, consider a situation in which there is inflation of 5 %. In that case an extra 10 % will not be sufficient to give the investor the same power to consume. If the investor wants to achieve the same level of consumption as that given up in the present he will need € 100 × (1 + 0.05) = € 105 only because of rising prices. In addition, he will require € 105 × (1 + 0.1) = € 115.5. As can be seen in case of inflation we are faced with two rates of interest: There is a market or nominal interest rate of 15.5 % and a real or purchasing-power interest rate of 10 %. The relationship between these interest rates is: (1 + real interest rate) × (1 + inflation rate) = (1 + nominal interest rate).

To move forward we must define which interest rate should be used in a net present value investment appraisal analysis. It is obvious that the net present value which is calculated for a given stream of cash flows would be significantly affected by the interest rates applied. Either interest rate will generate the same net present value for the project if the cash flows included in the investment appraisal have also been adjusted. If the cash flows have been estimated without taking into account the effects of inflation, then the real rate of interest should be taken. If they have been calculated taking into account the effects of inflation, then the nominal rate of interest should be used. The use of either method is acceptable. This is illustrated in the following comparison of alternatives.

5.3.2 Comparison of Alternatives

Table 5-6 shows the basic data which we always used to compare the alternatives.

Table 5-6 Basic data for the calculation of the net present values without inflation

	AK Rasant	SM Samurai
Initial outlay	9,000	14,000
Present value of an annuity	1.8594	2.7232
Cash flow per period	7,400	8,100
Net present value	4,760	8,058
Difference between net present values		3,298

With a discount rate of 5 % the net present value of the SM Samurai equals € 8,058 and therefore, it exceeds the net present value of the AK Rasant by € 3,298. Now, we assume 3.8 % inflation. To deal with inflation we recalculate the net present values using both approaches.

- Approach 1: Cash flows: Current value cash flows, Discount rate: Real rate of interest

Using this approach we merely show our usual calculation in a form which can easily be compared to approach 2. Hence, this is done for arithmetical convenience. The small differences to our earlier calculation are due to rounding errors because four-figure annuity present value factors were used.

For the AK Rasant we get:

$$\text{NPV} = €\,{-}9{,}000 + \frac{€\,7{,}400}{1.05} + \frac{€\,7{,}400}{1.05^2} = €\,{-}9{,}000 + €\,7{,}047.62 + €\,6{,}712.02 = €\,4{,}759.64$$

For the SM Samurai we get:

$$\text{NPV} = €\,{-}14{,}000 + \frac{€\,8{,}100}{1.05} + \frac{€\,8{,}100}{1.05^2} + \frac{€\,8{,}100}{1.05^3}$$

$$= €\,{-}14{,}000 + €\,7{,}714.29 + €\,7{,}346.94 + €\,6{,}997.24 = €\,8{,}058.47$$

- Approach 2: Cash flows: Actual cash flows, Discount rate: Nominal rate of interest

Using this approach we adjust the cash flows by the inflation rate and use as discount rate the nominal interest rate which is $(1 + 0.05) \times (1 + 0.038) = 1{,}09$.

For the AK Rasant we get:

$$\text{NPV} = €\,{-}9{,}000 + \frac{€7{,}681.2}{1.09} + \frac{€7{,}973.09}{1.09^2} = €\,{-}9{,}000 + €\,7{,}046.97 + €\,6{,}710.79 = €\,4{,}757.76$$

This is identical with the net present value of € 4,760 calculated earlier.

For the SM Samurai we get:

$$\text{NPV} = €\,{-}14{,}000 + \frac{€8{,}407.8}{1.09} + \frac{€8{,}727.3}{1.09^2} + \frac{€9{,}058.93}{1.09^3}$$

$$= €\,{-}14{,}000 + €\,7{,}713.58 + €\,7{,}345.59 + €\,6{,}995.31 = €\,8{,}054.48$$

This corresponds to the net present value of € 8,058 calculated earlier. The small differences are due to rounding errors because four-figure discount factors are used.

In calculating the two approaches, we showed that either approach is appropriate to calculate the net present value. However, in practice cash flows are not affected equally by inflation. Some cash flows like the savings from tax-allowable depreciation are even completely unaffected because they are based on the historical costs of the asset. Other cash flows may be partly affected. Then cash flow estimates in nominal terms (approach 2) is less erroneous because they can incorporate different inflationary trends. It follows that the nominal rate should be used as the appropriate discount rate.

5.3.3 Evaluation of Inflation

1. Inflation is defined as an increase in average prices. Failure to consider the impact of inflation can lead to an overestimation or underestimation of cash flows.

2. Be aware that inflation is not the same as the time value of money. To consider inflation is to make a calculation reflecting the project's cash flow in terms of purchasing power.

3. The relation between the interest rates is as described in the following formula:
$(1 + \text{real interest rate}) \times (1 + \text{inflation rate}) = (1 + \text{nominal interest rate})$

4. The presence of inflation can readily be addressed within the net present value approach of investment appraisal.

5. The net present value is usually calculated by using inflation adjusted cash flows and discounting these at the nominal rate of interest.

6. The decision maker must be careful not to mix up real values with nominal values because this would result in inaccurate data leading to detrimental advice.

5.4 Complete Financial Plan

5.4.1 Introduction

Up to this stage of the analysis, we have been examining the investment decision using one single interest rate, the market interest rate. In reality we know that the banking sector subsists on the difference between the borrowing and the lending interest rates. For the reason outlined in Chapter 3.3.2 we showed that all financing cash flows can be ignored when applying the net present value method. However, this was the case under the condition of identical debit interest rates and credit interest rates. At the discount rate we could lend money and reinvest it at any amount. Financial transactions within the economic life of the investment were possible at the discount rate. The reason was that there is no difference between saving money and getting credit interest or repaying loans and saving debit interest. The point of the net present value method is that there will be equal lending and borrowing interest rates as the result of a perfect capital market. Under these conditions investors are not faced with capital rationing.

In reality there is a gap between the borrowing and the lending interest rates. This means that there are two market interest rates. The interest rate depends on the term of a loan and on the reliability of the actors. Using the complete financial plan which was introduced in Chapter 3.3.2 we can model investment alternatives more precisely. The complete financial plan allows for consideration of various financing conditions and investment possibilities within the calculation.

5.4.2 Comparison of Alternatives

The data in Table 5-7 is repeated from Table 3-16. Again, we refer to the example from the comparison of alternatives using the net present value method.

Table 5-7 Basic data to set up a complete financial plan

	AK Rasant	SM Samurai
Initial outlay	9,000	14,000
Present value of an annuity	1.8594	2.7232
Cash flow per period	7,400	8,100
Net present value	4,760	8,058
Difference between net present values		3,298

First we set up a complete financial plan for the SM Samurai in Table 5-8 according to this information. In doing so, we first leave the assumption unchanged that the borrowing and lending rates are identical. Thus, the discount rate is uniformly 5 %. The investment is entirely financed through debt capital, assuming repayment in three equal rates.

Table 5-8 Complete financial plan for the SM Samurai at a discount rate of 5 %

Time period	0	1	2	3
Project cash flow	-14,000	8,100	8,100	8,100
Equity				
Debt				
+ Additional raise of loan	14,000			
- Loan repayment		-4,667	-4,667	-4,667
- Debit interest		-700	-467	-233
Deposit				
- Additional investment		-2,733	-5,837	-9,329
+ Repayment of money invested			2,733	5,837
+ Credit interest			137	292
Inventory				
Debt	14,000	9,333	4,667	0
Deposit	0	2,733	5,837	9,329
Balance	-14,000	-6,600	1,170	9,329

The terminal value of the investment taken from the cell 'Balance' is € 9,329. It can be discounted over 3 periods at 5 % (PVF 0.8638) and we get exactly the already identified net present value of € 8,058. This calculation should improve our understanding of the complete financial plan.

5.4 Complete Financial Plan

Now however, we change our assumptions about financing the investment. Again we assume a complete financing through loans. The negotiated debit interest rate is 6 %. Additional investments can be made at 5 %. In Table 5-9 we set up a complete financial plan under these new conditions. Hence, we know before calculating that the terminal value goes down in comparison to the former calculations because now a higher debit interest rate has to be paid.

Table 5-9 Complete financial plan for the SM Samurai with a debit interest rate of 6 % and a credit interest rate of 5 %

Time period	0	1	2	3
Project cash flow	-14,000	8,100	8,100	8,100
Equity				
Debt				
+ Additional raise of loan	14,000			
- Loan repayment		-4,667	-4,667	-4,667
- Debit interest		-840	-560	-280
Deposit				
- Additional investment		-2,593	-5,596	-9,029
+ Repayment of money invested			2,593	5,596
+ Credit interest			130	280
Inventory				
Debt	14,000	9,333	4,667	0
Deposit	0	2,593	5,596	9,029
Balance	-14,000	-6,740	930	9,029

5.4.3 Evaluation of the Complete Financial Plan

1. The assumptions about the financing of an investment become clear.
2. The complexity of conditions on the capital market is demonstrated.
3. The decision criterion is a future value at the end of the asset's economic life which can be readily understood.
4. It is problematic that financing actions cannot be attributed to single investment projects.
5. It is difficult to distinguish between project cash flows and financing cash flows.

5.5 Scoring Model

5.5.1 Introduction

Having examined the methods of investment appraisal with monetary input variables, it is now time to turn to a technique which can be of use when cash flows associated with the purchase of the investment are of a non-tangible nature. Thereby the investment possibilities are assessed under consideration of various criteria and ranked by a subjective order of preferences. This can be done by allocating scores to the alternatives according to their contribution to the company's business objective. Considering a subjective weighting these scores are added to a total value, the value of benefit. The total value of benefit calculated in this manner is not a monetary variable, as e.g. the net present value, but without dimension. Options can be ranked by the scoring model.

Scoring models are set up as follows:

1. Identifying assessment criteria: We must define assessment criteria that are useful for the project's appraisal. In doing so we must make sure that the criteria are not dependent on each other.

2. Contribution of weighting factors to these assessment criteria: Because the assessment criteria are not equally weighted we define weighting factors.

3. Choice of parameter values for the assessment criteria: We could use a scale from 0 to 10, in which 0 does not contribute to the company's objective and 10 makes a very good contribution.[32]

4. Assessment of the alternatives: Assessment of the alternatives is made by experts. They determine what contribution to the company's objective is made by each alternative.

5. Calculation of the values of benefit and ranking of alternatives: In the last step the calculation must be made. We calculate the total values of benefit which are used to rank the alternatives.

---

[32] For further approaches to convert contributions to business objectives in scores cf. Blohm, Hans, Klaus Lüder and Christina Schaefer, Investition, op. cit., pp. 161-165.

5.5.2 Comparison of Alternatives

We implement the scoring model for the comparison of alternatives:

- To 1) Identify assessment criteria

To choose the right vehicle we identify the following assessment criteria:

- Profitability
- Driving Performance
- Spaciousness
- Representativity

- To 2) Contribution of weighting factors to these assessment criteria

- Profitability: 60 %
- Driving Performance: 20 %
- Spaciousness: 10 %
- Representativity: 10 %

- To 3) Choice of parameter values for the assessment criteria

We choose the assessment criterion 'representativity' as an example. The contributions to benefit are shown in Table 5-10.

Table 5-10 Contributions of the assessment criterion 'representativity'

Points	Contribution to the objective
0	not representative
1–3	lower representativity
4–6	middle representativity
7–10	high representativity

- To 4) Assessment of the alternatives

Assessing the alternatives lead to partial values of benefit as shown in Table 5-11.

Table 5-11 Partial values of benefit for the alternatives under consideration

	Model AK Rasant	Model SM Samurai
Profitability	6	8
Driving Performance	4	3
Spaciousness	4	4
Representativity	5	4

- To 5) Calculation of the values of benefit and ranking of alternatives

Table 5-12 Total values for the alternatives considered

Alternatives		Model AK Rasant		Model SM Samurai	
Assessment criterion	Weighting factor	Partial utility	Value of benefit	Partial utility	Value of benefit
Profitability	0.6	6	3.6	8	4.8
Driving Performance	0.2	4	0.8	3	0.6
Spaciousness	0.1	4	0.4	4	0.4
Representativity	0.1	5	0.5	4	0.4
Total value			5.3		6.2
Rank			2		1

From Table 5-12 we see that the SM Samurai is better than the AK Rasant, because it has the higher total value of benefit. This is mainly due to the high weighting factor of the assessment criterion profitability. Indeed, we can see that this result is subjective but the relatively complex decision problem has been structured reasonably and the decision has become clear.

5.5.3 Evaluation of the Scoring Model

1. Scoring models provide clearness in complex investment decisions.

2. They are widely applicable and easy to communicate.

3. Scoring models are especially useful if it is not possible to quantify the investment's cash flow.

4. Due to the high degree of subjectivity the derived results depend on those carrying out the analysis.

5. It is important that the assessment criteria do not depend on each other. Otherwise the addition of single values of benefit would not be useful because of duplication of the data.

6. The determination of assessment criteria and the designation of weighting factors for these assessment criteria are problematic.

7. Indeed, the condensing of all information into one single value of benefit leads to a better overview of the decision problem, but also to a loss of information if, for example, one of the alternatives performs extremely badly in one criterion.

5.6 Macroeconomic Net Present Value Method

5.6.1 Introduction

Investment appraisal techniques are also used in the public sector. These are macroeconomic investment appraisal techniques that take into account all effects from the realisation of an investment project. So far we have been considering only internal effects of an investment. Internal or direct influences affect those who realise the investment. These are generally monetary influences, but using a scoring model also allows the consideration of non-monetary effects in investment appraisals.[33]

In this section we will learn how to take into account external effects outside the project executing organisation. These are effects on people or institutions apart from those who realise the investment. These effects are called indirect or external effects. If they are positive they are called indirect utility, whereas if they are negative they are called indirect costs. Macroeconomic investment appraisal techniques are necessary to assess investments within the public sector.[34] These are e.g. the construction of a new road which produces time sav-

---

[33] For macroeconomic scoring models cf. Blohm, Hans, Klaus Lüder, and Christina Schaefer, Investition, op. cit., pp. 178-185.

[34] Public budget laws demand evaluation of economic efficiency explicitly. According to state and federal budgetary regulations (Section 6 Paragraph 2 Haushaltsgrundsätzegesetz and Section 7 Paragraph 2 Bundeshaushalt-

ings for some parts of the population but noise pollution for others. Supplies for the local music school do not only cost money, but also lead to a higher level of education of its users. The improvement of a pedestrian zone enhances its attractiveness and therefore encourages employment in neighbouring shops.

Basically a macroeconomic cost-benefit-analysis does not differ from a normal net present value approach. However, all effects from the investment are taken into consideration, those arising directly by the project executing organisation as well as the external effects influencing others. The decision criterion using investment appraisal techniques for public investments is the macroeconomic net present value NPV^M, that is, the difference between the present value of all utilities and the present value of all costs. Here we use monetary units for all effects of the investment. If that is not possible, then these effects have to be listed separately.

The decision criteria for the macroeconomic net present value method are:

- A single investment would be preferable if its macroeconomic net present value is positive. This means: $NPV^M > 0$.

- In the context of mutually exclusive investments, then an investment 1 is better than an investment 2 if its macroeconomic net present value is greater.
This means: $NPV_1^M > NPV_2^M$.

We can get a good overview of the macroeconomic effects if we first pursue a microeconomic investment appraisal from the investor's point of view and then a macroeconomic investment appraisal.

---

sordnung) for all financial actions appropriate economic feasibility studies have to be performed. Analogous rules can be found in the various regulations for local authority budgets.

5.6.2 Comparison of Alternatives

Using the microeconomic net present value approach we have been calculating the following net present values (Table 5-13).

Table 5-13 Basic data for the macroeconomic net present value method

	AK Rasant	SM Samurai
Initial outlay	9,000	14,000
Present value of an annuity	1.8594	2.7232
Cash flow per period	7,400	8,100
Net present value	4,760	8,058
Difference between net present values		3,298

We considered both alternatives to be worthwhile because of their positive net present value. We chose the SM Samurai because its net present value is higher by € 3,298.

For a macroeconomic consideration we include the following aspects to our calculation:

- The customers of the car sharing company will use the already existing tram less frequently. The local public transportation supplier will suffer losses in its revenues of € 3,500.
- The SM Samurai is located in a public street next to a kindergarten which is troubled by automobile traffic. It is not possible to quantify this disadvantage.
- The female users of the car sharing company appreciate the higher security in the evenings because in case of late classes they can drive home directly by car and avoid the lonely way to the tram. This advantage is quantified at € 500 per year.

In Table 5-14 we calculate the macroeconomic net present value using the information.

Table 5-14 Calculation of the macroeconomic net present value

	AK Rasant	SM Samurai
Initial outlay	-9,000	-14,000
Present value of an annuity	1.8594	2.7232
Microeconomic cash flow per period	7,400	8,100
Losses in public transportation per period	-3,500	-3,500
Increase in security per period	500	500
Net present value	-819	-112

From a macroeconomic point of view the investment is no longer worthwhile because both net present values are negative. Furthermore, the disadvantage, that the kindergarten is disturbed by the noise, has not yet been taken explicitly into consideration. For the assessment of the investment's desirability the disadvantage must be considered. It downgrades the investment project further. Using a scoring model allows the consideration of this disadvantage explicitly by an investment appraisal technique.

5.6.3 Evaluation of the Macroeconomic Net Present Value Method

1. Macroeconomic investment appraisal techniques lead to considerable manipulation margins, because the generated utilities have to be expressed in monetary units.

2. Problems can arise if the appropriate discount rate has to be chosen.

3. Generally it is not possible to generate clear results.

4. However, macroeconomic investment appraisals help the decision maker because they make all assessment clear and understandable.

5. Generally, the decision over the implementation of a macroeconomic investment is a political decision.

5.7 Summary and Evaluation

In the first chapters of this book you became acquainted with non-discounting and discounting methods to justify capital expenditures. The point of the whole analysis is to judge whether the company will be better off or worse off if it undertakes the project. You have been learning the advantages and disadvantages of the various approaches. Thus, you should be familiar with applying the appropriate method for the respective problem in capital budgeting. This is of great importance for the existence of a company because capital expenditures are long-term and bind a large amount of capital.

Usually the justification of capital expenditures will be made by computing a net present value. This is the most widely recommended method of capital investment analysis. Therefore you carefully estimate expected future cash flows of the investment. Project evaluation rests upon incremental cash flows. This cash flow would disappear if the project disappeared. The net present value is an unambiguous value which provides definite decision advice for investments. In the forth chapter you learned what to do when certainty is replaced by only expectation: Identify risk and uncertainties and at least run a sensitivity analysis. Finally this chapter made clear how important it was to use the same example for all presented methods of investment appraisal. By that time you knew the initial data nearly by heart and therefore were able to concentrate on the differences between the presented techniques.

In this fifth and last chapter we have been integrating further aspects to derive more advanced solutions. You should be able to adapt your calculations to taxation as well as inflation and particularities regarding the financing of the investment. If non-monetary influencing factors occur, then a scoring model would support the investment decision. Finally, with the macroeconomic net present value method, you learned a method of investment appraisal for public investments.

The methods presented in this book do not guarantee the success of the investment project. Opting for any model begs the question of how the complex real world can be represented by a model. But the decision maker is enabled to undertake an investment on the basis of an informed decision. The investment appraisal techniques present a structure for evaluating, comparing and ranking the alternative investment projects. They can not tell a decision maker to invest or not to invest, but they act as a good decision guide. Investment appraisal techniques can never replace managerial judgement, but they can help to make the judgement sounder.

5.8 Exercises with Answers

5.8.1 Exercises

Exercise 5-1 Net present value method and taxation

A farmer is concerned about the modernisation of his equipment. He considers if it makes sense to purchase so-called milking robots. This complicated technical equipment consists of a box regulated by a bar which allows entry of one cow at a time. The teats are automatically addressed by laser rays. The cow is milked exactly as long as there is a steady flow of milk. This can be beneficial to the health of the herd because the milking log reveals helpful information about each cow. In addition, the farmer can halve his milking time.

Such a milking robot costs € 120,000 and presumably has an estimated economic life of 20 years. Annual repair costs are € 200. Every year the following costs can be saved: € 9,000 for personnel and € 1,000 for veterinary examinations because the cows get ill from inflammation of the udder less frequently. All payments with the exception of the initial outlay occur at the end of the respective year. The discount rate is 5 %.

a) Compute the net present value of the investment, and state whether the investment is worthwhile. Ignore taxation.

b) Now, calculate the net present value using a 30 percent tax rate. How does this change your results?

Exercise 5-2 Net present value method and inflation

A company considers purchasing a machine for € 6,000 at the beginning of year 1. It has a three-year economic life and will reduce annual labour expenses by € 2,700. The investors' expectations of inflation are included in the required rate of return which is 10 %. Inflation is 4 %. Is this an attractive investment? Compute the net present value ignoring inflation first (a) and then recognising inflation (b) to show that choosing the appropriate cash flows and discount rate will lead to the same net present value.

Exercise 5-3 Complete financial plan

The following situation describes two investment alternatives:

	AK Rasant	SM Samurai
Initial outlay	9,000	14,000
PVA	1.8594	2.7232
Cash flow per period	7,400	8,100
Net present value	4,760	8,058
Difference between net present values		3,298

Set up a complete financial plan for the investment of the SM Samurai under the following conditions: The investment is financed with € 5,000 equity, the difference is financed by a loan at 6 %, credit interest 5 %. The repayment of the loan occurs at three equal annual rates, beginning at the end of the first year.

Exercise 5-4 Scoring model

After three successful periods, the car sharing company considers expanding its business. In order to extend the variety of products, the company considers purchasing either another SM Samurai or a sports utility vehicle of Lord Pioneer.

The following limitations are crucial:

- The heavy utility vehicles are characterised by high gas consumption.
- The positive image and the good-looking outfit might attract customers besides students.
- The relatively high cost should not result in respective pricing, but prices should be maintained at a moderate level.

5.8 Exercises with Answers

Assume the following decision criteria and weighting factors:

- Profitability: 60 %
- Driving Performance: 20 %
- Spaciousness: 10 %
- Representativity: 10 %

For each assessment criterion we define contributions to the company's objective from 0 (criterion not fulfilled) to 10 (criterion very well fulfilled). Here are the results:

	SM Samurai	Lord Pioneer
Profitability	8	2
Driving Performance	3	9
Spaciousness	4	8
Representativity	4	9

Finish the scoring model and rank the alternatives.

Exercise 5-5 Macroeconomic net present value method

A local transportation authority is considering the prolongation of a tramway in order to connect a new residential area to the local transportation system. Until now the area could be reached only very circuitously by a single accommodation road. These are the planned financial details:

- Construction costs € 20 Mio. A government grant of € 4 Mio. is expected. The economic life is supposed to be 30 years.
- Maintenance costs are € 0.2 Mio. per year.
- Revenues from the users of the new tramway € 0.5 Mio. per year.
- Saved costs for accidents: € 1 Mio. per year.
- Time saving, valued with € 0.6 Mio. per year.

a) First run a normal investment appraisal calculation from the project executing organisation's point of view. To reach this aim, use the net present value method at a 5 % discount rate. If necessary, round to whole Euros. All payments occur at the end of each year.

b) Then set up a macroeconomic net present value approach that incurs the project's external effects. Check if this changes the desirability of the tramway's prolongation.

5.8.2 Answers

Answer to exercise 5-1 Net present value method and taxation

a)

Initial outlay	120,000
PVA (20 years, 5 %)	12.4622
Cash flow per year	9,800
Net present value	2,130

The net present value is positive and consequently the investment project acceptable.

b) Computing the cash flow after tax:

Cash flow before tax	9,800
- Depreciation	6,000
= Taxable income	3,800
- Tax payable	1,140
= Income after tax	2,660
+ Depreciation	6,000
= After tax cash flow	8,660

Calculation of the net present value:

Initial outlay	120,000
PVA (20 years, 3.5 %)	14.2124
After tax cash flow	8,660
Net present value	3,079

The discount rate falls to 3.5 % = 0.05 × (1–0.3).

The investment is still attractive because its net present value is above zero. In addition, the net present value after tax exceeds the one before tax. This can be explained by the so-called tax paradox.

Answer to exercise 5-2 Net present value method and inflation

a) Ignoring inflation

$$\text{NPV} = \text{€ -6,000} + \frac{\text{€ 2,700}}{1.1} + \frac{\text{€ 2,700}}{1.1^2} + \frac{\text{€ 2,700}}{1.1^3}$$

= € -6,000 + € 2,454.55 + € 2,231.40 + € 2,028.55 = € 714.50

b) Recognising inflation

Now we adjust the cash flows by the inflation rate and use as discount rate the nominal interest rate which is: $(1 + 0.1) \times (1 + 0.04) = 1.144$.

$$\text{NPV} = \text{€ -6,000} + \frac{\text{€ 2,808}}{1.144} + \frac{\text{€ 2,920.32}}{1.144^2} + \frac{\text{€ 3,037.13}}{1.144^3}$$

= € -6,000 + € 2,454.55 + € 2,231.47 + € 2,028.54 = € 714.56

Differences are due to rounding errors because four-figure values are used.

We showed that the net present value is the same using either approach. The net present value is positive and hence the investment is attractive.

Answer to exercise 5-3 Complete financial plan

Time period	0	1	2	3
Project cash flow	-14,000	8,100	8,100	8,100
Equity	5,000			
Debt				
+ Additional raise of loan	9,000			
- Loan repayment		-3,000	-3,000	-3,000
- Debit interest		-540	-360	-180
Deposit				
- Additional investment		-4,560	-9,528	-14,924
+ Repayment of money invested			4,560	9,528
+ Credit interest			228	476
Inventory				
Debt	9,000	6,000	3,000	0
Deposit	0	4,560	9,528	14,924
Balance	-9,000	-1,440	6,528	14,924

Answer to exercise 5-4 Scoring model

Alternatives		SM Samurai		Lord Pionier	
Assessment criterion	Weighting factor	Partial utility	Value of benefit	Partial utility	Value of benefit
Profitability	0.6	8	4.8	2	1.2
Driving performance	0.2	3	0.6	9	1.8
Spaciousness	0.1	4	0.4	8	0.8
Representativity	0.1	4	0.4	9	0.9
Total value			6.2		4.7
Rank			1		2

We can observe that the purchase of the sports utility vehicle is not desirable as long as the assessment criterion profitability has a high weighting factor, but the sports utility vehicle gets only relatively low scores in that respect.

Answer to exercise 5-5 Macroeconomic net present value method

a)

Construction costs: € 20 Mio. – grant of € 4 Mio.	€ 16,000,000
+ Maintenance: € 200,000 × PVA (5 %, 30 y.) 15.3725	€ 3,074,500
= Present value of all cash outflow	€ 19,074,500
Present value of all cash inflow: € 500,000 × PVA (5 %, 30 y.) 15.3725	€ 7,686,250
– Present value of all cash outflow:	€ 19,074,500
= Net present value	€ –11,388,250

Thus, for the local transportation company the investment would not be worthwhile.

b)

Within a macroeconomic investment appraisal the total costs of investment, including the grant, have to be taken into account. The present value of all cash outflows rises by these € 4 Mio. to € 23,074,500.

Within a macroeconomic investment appraisal the revenues of the local transportation company are not considered in the calculation because these payments are made by the users. From a macroeconomic point of view these payments cancel each other out.

Instead we get:

Benefit of lower costs of accidents: € 1 Mio. × PVA (5 %, 30 y.) 15.3725	€ 15,372,500
+ Benefit of travel time: € 0.6 Mio. × PVA (5 %, 30 y.) 15.3725	€ 9,223,500
Present value of all benefits	€ 24,596,000
Present value of all benefits:	€ 24,596,000
– Present value of all costs:	€ 23,074,500
= Net present value	€ 1,521,500

However, from a macroeconomic point of view the investment is worthwhile.

6 Index of Questions and Solutions

Exercise 1-1 Connection between investment and financing 5
Exercise 1-2 Investment and financing with their performance in the balance sheet and the profit and loss account 6
Exercise 1-3 Types of investments 6
Exercise 1-4 Investment appraisal 6
Exercise 2-1 Cost comparison method – Comparison of alternatives 39
Exercise 2-2 Cost comparison method – Comparison of alternatives with salvage values 39
Exercise 2-3 Cost comparison method – Comparison of alternatives with critical values 40
Exercise 2-4 Cost comparison method – Replacement decision 40
Exercise 2-5 Profit comparison method – Comparison of alternatives 41
Exercise 2-6 Profit comparison method – Comparison of alternatives with critical values ... 41
Exercise 2-7 Profit comparison method – Replacement decision 42
Exercise 2-8 Accounting rate of return method – Comparison of alternatives 43
Exercise 2-9 Accounting rate of return method – Replacement decision 43
Exercise 2-10 Accounting rate of return method and payback method – Comparison of alternatives 43
Exercise 2-11 Payback method – Replacement decision 44
Exercise 2-12 Diverse methods of non-discounting investment appraisal 44
Exercise 3-1 Basics of the discounting methods of investment appraisal 90
Exercise 3-2 Net present value method I 91
Exercise 3-3 Net present value method II 91
Exercise 3-4 Net present value method III 91
Exercise 3-5 Net present value method IV 92
Exercise 3-6 Net present value method V 92
Exercise 3-7 Cost comparison method and net present value method 93
Exercise 3-8 Annuity method 94
Exercise 3-9 Internal rate of return method 94

Exercise 3-10 Accounting rate of return method and internal rate of return method 94
Exercise 3-11 Non-discounting and discounting methods of investment appraisal 95
Exercise 4-1 Investment decision making under uncertainty – Correction method 135
Exercise 4-2 Investment decision making under uncertainty – Sensitivity analysis 136
Exercise 4-3 Investment decision making under uncertainty – Risk analysis 137
Exercise 4-4 Investment decision making under uncertainty – Decision tree analysis:
 flexible planning 138
Exercise 5-1 Net present value method and taxation 167
Exercise 5-2 Net present value method and inflation 168
Exercise 5-3 Complete financial plan 168
Exercise 5-4 Scoring model 168
Exercise 5-5 Macroeconomic net present value method 169

Answer to exercise 1-1 Connection between investment and financing 7
Answer to exercise 1-2 Investment and financing with their performance
 in the balance sheet and the profit and loss account 7
Answer to exercise 1-3 Types of investments 8
Answer to exercise 1-4 Investment appraisal 9
Answer to exercise 2-1 Cost comparison method – Comparison of alternatives 45
Answer to exercise 2-2 Cost comparison method – Comparison of alternatives
 with salvage values 46
Answer to exercise 2-3 Cost comparison method – Comparison of alternatives
 with critical values 46
Answer to exercise 2-4 Cost comparison method – Replacement decision 47
Answer to exercise 2-5 Profit comparison method – Comparison of alternatives 48
Answer to exercise 2-6 Profit comparison method – Comparison of alternatives
 with critical values 48
Answer to exercise 2-7 Profit comparison method – Replacement decision 49
Answer to exercise 2-8 Accounting rate of return method – Comparison of alternatives 50
Answer to exercise 2-9 Accounting rate of return method – Replacement decision 50
Answer to exercise 2-10 Accounting rate of return method and payback method –
 Comparison of alternatives 51
Answer to exercise 2-11 Payback method – Replacement decision 52
Answer to exercise 2-12 Diverse methods of non-discounting investment appraisal 53
Answer to exercise 3-1 Basics of the discounting methods of investment appraisal 95

6 Index of Questions and Solutions

Answer to exercise 3-2 Net present value method I 96
Answer to exercise 3-3 Net present value method II 97
Answer to exercise 3-4 Net present value method III 97
Answer to exercise 3-5 Net present value method IV 98
Answer to exercise 3-6 Net present value method V 100
Answer to exercise 3-7 Cost comparison method and net present value method 101
Answer to exercise 3-8 Annuity method 102
Answer to exercise 3-9 Internal rate of return method 102
Answer to exercise 3-10 Accounting rate of return method and internal rate
    of return method 104
Answer to exercise 3-11 Non-discounting and discounting methods
    of investment appraisal 105
Answer to exercise 4-1 Investment decision making under uncertainty –
    correction method 140
Answer to exercise 4-2 Investment decision making under uncertainty –
    sensitivity analysis 142
Answer to exercise 4-3 Investment decision making under uncertainty – risk analysis 144
Answer to exercise 4-4 Investment decision making under uncertainty –
    decision tree analysis: flexible planning 146
Answer to exercise 5-1 Net present value method and taxation 170
Answer to exercise 5-2 Net present value method and inflation 171
Answer to exercise 5-3 Complete financial plan 171
Answer to exercise 5-4 Scoring model 172
Answer to exercise 5-5 Macroeconomic net present value method 172

7 References

Adam, Dietrich, Investitionscontrolling, 3rd ed., München 2000.

Anthony, Martin, and Norman Biggs, Mathematics for Economics and Finance: Methods and Modelling, 11th ed., Cambridge 2005.

Bierman, Harold, and Seymour Smidt, The Capital Budgeting Decision: Economic Analysis of Investment Projects, 8th ed., Upper Saddle River 1993.

Blohm, Hans, Klaus Lüder and Christina Schaefer, Investition, 9th ed., München 2006.

Brealey, Richard A., Steward C. Myers and Alan J. Marcus, Fundamentals of Corporate Finance, 5th ed., New York 2006.

Capinski, Marek, and Tomasz Zastawniak, Mathematics for Finance: An Introduction to Financial Engineering, London 2003.

Däumler, Klaus-Dieter, Grundlagen der Investitions- und Wirtschaftlichkeitsrechnung, 11th ed., Herne/Berlin 2003.

Dayananda, Don, et al., Capital Budgeting: Financial Appraisal of Investment Projects, Cambridge 2002.

Götze, Uwe, Investitionsrechnung: Modelle und Analysen zur Beurteilung von Investitionsvorhaben, 5th ed., Berlin 2005.

Gräfer, Horst, Rolf Beike and Guido A. Scheld, Finanzierung, 5th ed., Berlin 2001.

Grob, Heinz Lothar, Einführung in die Investitionsrechnung, 5th ed., München 2006.

Günther, Peter, and Frank Andreas Schittenhelm, Investition und Finanzierung: Eine Einführung in das Finanz- und Risikomanagement, Stuttgart 2003.

Hoffmeister, Wolfgang, Investitionsrechnung und Nutzwertanalyse: Eine entscheidungsorientierte Darstellung mit vielen Beispielen und Übungen, Stuttgart 2000.

Holmes, Phil, Investment Appraisal, London 1998.

Homann, Klaus, Kommunales Rechnungswesen: Buchführung, Kostenrechnung und Wirtschaftlichkeitsrechnung, 6th ed., Wiesbaden 2005.

Jahrmann, Fritz-Ulrich, Finanzierung, 5th ed., Herne/Berlin 2003.

Jones, Charles P., Investments: Analysis and Management, 9th ed., Hoboken 2004.

Kruschwitz, Lutz, Finanzierung und Investition, 4th ed., München 2004.

Kruschwitz, Lutz, Investitionsrechnung, 10th ed., München 2005.

Lumby, Steve, and Chris Jones, Corporate Finance: Theory and Practice, 7th ed., London 2003.

Lumby, Steve, and Chris Jones, Fundamentals of Investment Appraisal, London 2001.

Manz, Klaus, et al., Investition, Kompaktstudium Wirtschaftswissenschaften Bd. 5, 2nd ed., München 1999.

Mayo, Herbert B., Investments: An Introduction, 7th ed., Mason 2003.

Melicher, Ronald W., and Edgar A. Norton, Finance: Introduction to Institutions, Investments, and Management, 12th ed., Hoboken 2005.

Olfert, Klaus, and Christopher Reichel, Finanzierung, 13th ed., Ludwigshafen 2005.

Olfert, Klaus, and Christopher Reichel, Investition, 10th ed., Ludwigshafen 2006.

Peterson, Pamela P., and Frank J. Fabozzi, Capital Budgeting: Theory and Practice, Hoboken 2002.

Pflaumer, Peter, Investitionsrechnung, 5th ed., München 2004.

Röhrich, Martina, Wirtschaftlichkeitsanalysen kommunaler Investitionen am Beispiel Eigentum versus Miete: Ein Plädoyer für die gesetzliche Festschreibung der Kapitalwertmethode, in: Zeitschrift für Kommunalfinanzen 44 (1994), pp. 4-8.

Röhrich, Martina, Contracting, in: Das Wirtschaftsstudium 26 (1997), p. 312.

Röhrich, Martina, Finanzierung öffentlicher EDV-Rationalisierungsinvestitionen durch Leasing, in: Der Gemeindehaushalt 98 (1997), pp. 152-159.

Rolfes, Bernd, Moderne Investitionsrechnung, 3rd ed., München 2003.

Ross, Stephen A., Randolph W. Westerfield and Bradford D. Jordan, Corporate Finance: Essentials, 5th ed., New York 2006.

Seitz, Neil, and Mitch Ellison, Capital Budgeting and Long-Term Financing Decisions, 4th ed., Mason 2005.

Shapiro, Alan C., Capital Budgeting and Investment Analysis, Upper Saddle River 2004.

Swoboda, Peter, Investition und Finanzierung: Betriebswirtschaftslehre im Grundstudium der Wirtschaftswissenschaft, Bd. 3, 5th ed., Göttingen 1996.

Wöhe, Günter, Einführung in die Allgemeine Betriebswirtschaftslehre, 22th ed., München 2005.

Wöhe, Günter, Hans Kaiser and Ulrich Döring, Übungsbuch zur Einführung in die Allgemeine Betriebswirtschaftslehre, 11th ed., München 2005.

8 Mathematical Tables

Future Value Factor

Number of Periods	3.0%	3.5%	4.0%	4.5%	5.0%	5.5%	6.0%	6.5%	7.0%	7.5%	8.0%	8.5%	9.0%	9.5%	10.0%
1	1.0300	1.0350	1.0400	1.0450	1.0500	1.0550	1.0600	1.0650	1.0700	1.0750	1.0800	1.0850	1.0900	1.0950	1.1000
2	1.0609	1.0712	1.0816	1.0920	1.1025	1.1130	1.1236	1.1342	1.1449	1.1556	1.1664	1.1772	1.1881	1.1990	1.2100
3	1.0927	1.1087	1.1249	1.1412	1.1576	1.1742	1.1910	1.2079	1.2250	1.2423	1.2597	1.2773	1.2950	1.3129	1.3310
4	1.1255	1.1475	1.1699	1.1925	1.2155	1.2388	1.2625	1.2865	1.3108	1.3355	1.3605	1.3859	1.4116	1.4377	1.4641
5	1.1593	1.1877	1.2167	1.2462	1.2763	1.3070	1.3382	1.3701	1.4026	1.4356	1.4693	1.5037	1.5386	1.5742	1.6105
6	1.1941	1.2293	1.2653	1.3023	1.3401	1.3788	1.4185	1.4591	1.5007	1.5433	1.5869	1.6315	1.6771	1.7238	1.7716
7	1.2299	1.2723	1.3159	1.3609	1.4071	1.4547	1.5036	1.5540	1.6058	1.6590	1.7138	1.7701	1.8280	1.8876	1.9487
8	1.2668	1.3168	1.3686	1.4221	1.4775	1.5347	1.5938	1.6550	1.7182	1.7835	1.8509	1.9206	1.9926	2.0669	2.1436
9	1.3048	1.3629	1.4233	1.4861	1.5513	1.6191	1.6895	1.7626	1.8385	1.9172	1.9990	2.0839	2.1719	2.2632	2.3579
10	1.3439	1.4106	1.4802	1.5530	1.6289	1.7081	1.7908	1.8771	1.9672	2.0610	2.1589	2.2610	2.3674	2.4782	2.5937
11	1.3842	1.4600	1.5395	1.6229	1.7103	1.8021	1.8983	1.9992	2.1049	2.2156	2.3316	2.4532	2.5804	2.7137	2.8531
12	1.4258	1.5111	1.6010	1.6959	1.7959	1.9012	2.0122	2.1291	2.2522	2.3818	2.5182	2.6617	2.8127	2.9715	3.1384
13	1.4685	1.5640	1.6651	1.7722	1.8856	2.0058	2.1329	2.2675	2.4098	2.5604	2.7196	2.8879	3.0658	3.2537	3.4523
14	1.5126	1.6187	1.7317	1.8519	1.9799	2.1161	2.2609	2.4149	2.5785	2.7524	2.9372	3.1334	3.3417	3.5629	3.7975
15	1.5580	1.6753	1.8009	1.9353	2.0789	2.2325	2.3966	2.5718	2.7590	2.9589	3.1722	3.3997	3.6425	3.9013	4.1772
16	1.6047	1.7340	1.8730	2.0224	2.1829	2.3553	2.5404	2.7390	2.9522	3.1808	3.4259	3.6887	3.9703	4.2719	4.5950
17	1.6528	1.7947	1.9479	2.1134	2.2920	2.4848	2.6928	2.9170	3.1588	3.4194	3.7000	4.0023	4.3276	4.6778	5.0545
18	1.7024	1.8575	2.0258	2.2085	2.4066	2.6215	2.8543	3.1067	3.3799	3.6758	3.9960	4.3425	4.7171	5.1222	5.5599
19	1.7535	1.9225	2.1068	2.3079	2.5270	2.7656	3.0256	3.3086	3.6165	3.9515	4.3157	4.7116	5.1417	5.6088	6.1159
20	1.8061	1.9898	2.1911	2.4117	2.6533	2.9178	3.2071	3.5236	3.8697	4.2479	4.6610	5.1120	5.6044	6.1416	6.7275
21	1.8603	2.0594	2.2788	2.5202	2.7860	3.0782	3.3996	3.7527	4.1406	4.5664	5.0338	5.5466	6.1088	6.7251	7.4002
22	1.9161	2.1315	2.3699	2.6337	2.9253	3.2475	3.6035	3.9966	4.4304	4.9089	5.4365	6.0180	6.6586	7.3639	8.1403
23	1.9736	2.2061	2.4647	2.7522	3.0715	3.4262	3.8197	4.2564	4.7405	5.2771	5.8715	6.5296	7.2579	8.0635	8.9543
24	2.0328	2.2833	2.5633	2.8760	3.2251	3.6146	4.0489	4.5331	5.0724	5.6729	6.3412	7.0846	7.9111	8.8296	9.8497
25	2.0938	2.3632	2.6658	3.0054	3.3864	3.8134	4.2919	4.8277	5.4274	6.0983	6.8485	7.6868	8.6231	9.6684	10.8347
26	2.1566	2.4460	2.7725	3.1407	3.5557	4.0231	4.5494	5.1415	5.8074	6.5557	7.3964	8.3401	9.3992	10.5869	11.9182
27	2.2213	2.5316	2.8834	3.2820	3.7335	4.2444	4.8223	5.4757	6.2139	7.0474	7.9881	9.0490	10.2451	11.5926	13.1100
28	2.2879	2.6202	2.9987	3.4297	3.9201	4.4778	5.1117	5.8316	6.6488	7.5759	8.6271	9.8182	11.1671	12.6939	14.4210
29	2.3566	2.7119	3.1187	3.5840	4.1161	4.7241	5.4184	6.2107	7.1143	8.1441	9.3173	10.6528	12.1722	13.8998	15.8631
30	2.4273	2.8068	3.2434	3.7453	4.3219	4.9840	5.7435	6.6144	7.6123	8.7550	10.0627	11.5583	13.2677	15.2203	17.4494

8 Mathematical Tables

Annuity Future Value Factor

Number of Periods	3.0%	3.5%	4.0%	4.5%	5.0%	5.5%	6.0%	6.5%	7.0%	7.5%	8.0%	8.5%	9.0%	9.5%	10.0%
1	1.0000	1.0000	1.0000	1.0000	1.0000	1.0000	1.0000	1.0000	1.0000	1.0000	1.0000	1.0000	1.0000	1.0000	1.0000
2	2.0300	2.0350	2.0400	2.0450	2.0500	2.0550	2.0600	2.0650	2.0700	2.0750	2.0800	2.0850	2.0900	2.0950	2.1000
3	3.0909	3.1062	3.1216	3.1370	3.1525	3.1680	3.1836	3.1992	3.2149	3.2306	3.2464	3.2622	3.2781	3.2940	3.3100
4	4.1836	4.2149	4.2465	4.2782	4.3101	4.3423	4.3746	4.4072	4.4399	4.4729	4.5061	4.5395	4.5731	4.6070	4.6410
5	5.3091	5.3625	5.4163	5.4707	5.5256	5.5811	5.6371	5.6936	5.7507	5.8084	5.8666	5.9254	5.9847	6.0446	6.1051
6	6.4684	6.5502	6.6330	6.7169	6.8019	6.8881	6.9753	7.0637	7.1533	7.2440	7.3359	7.4290	7.5233	7.6189	7.7156
7	7.6625	7.7794	7.8983	8.0192	8.1420	8.2669	8.3938	8.5229	8.6540	8.7873	8.9228	9.0605	9.2004	9.3426	9.4872
8	8.8923	9.0517	9.2142	9.3800	9.5491	9.7216	9.8975	10.0769	10.2598	10.4464	10.6366	10.8306	11.0285	11.2302	11.4359
9	10.1591	10.3685	10.5828	10.8021	11.0266	11.2563	11.4913	11.7319	11.9780	12.2298	12.4876	12.7512	13.0210	13.2971	13.5795
10	11.4639	11.7314	12.0061	12.2882	12.5779	12.8754	13.1808	13.4944	13.8164	14.1471	14.4866	14.8351	15.1929	15.5603	15.9374
11	12.8078	13.1420	13.4864	13.8412	14.2068	14.5835	14.9716	15.3716	15.7836	16.2081	16.6455	17.0961	17.5603	18.0385	18.5312
12	14.1920	14.6020	15.0258	15.4640	15.9171	16.3856	16.8699	17.3707	17.8885	18.4237	18.9771	19.5492	20.1407	20.7522	21.3843
13	15.6178	16.1130	16.6268	17.1599	17.7130	18.2868	18.8821	19.4998	20.1406	20.8055	21.4953	22.2109	22.9534	23.7236	24.5227
14	17.0863	17.6770	18.2919	18.9321	19.5986	19.2926	21.0151	21.7673	22.5505	23.3659	24.2149	25.0989	26.0192	26.9774	27.9750
15	18.5989	19.2957	20.0236	20.7841	21.5786	22.4087	23.2760	24.1822	25.1290	26.1184	27.1521	28.2323	29.3609	30.5402	31.7725
16	20.1569	20.9710	21.8245	22.7193	23.6575	24.6411	25.6725	26.7540	27.8881	29.0772	30.3243	31.6320	33.0034	34.4416	35.9497
17	21.7616	22.7050	23.6975	24.7417	25.8404	26.9964	28.2129	29.4930	30.8402	32.2580	33.7502	35.3207	36.9737	38.7135	40.5447
18	23.4144	24.4997	25.6454	26.8551	28.1324	29.4812	30.9057	32.4101	33.9990	35.6774	37.4502	39.3230	41.3013	43.3913	45.5992
19	25.1169	26.3572	27.6712	29.0636	30.5390	32.1027	33.7600	35.5167	37.3790	39.3532	41.4463	43.6654	46.0185	48.5135	51.1591
20	26.8704	28.2797	29.7781	31.3714	33.0660	34.8683	36.7856	38.8253	40.9955	43.3047	45.7620	48.3770	51.1601	54.1222	57.2750
21	28.6765	30.2695	31.9692	33.7831	35.7193	37.7861	39.9927	42.3490	44.8652	47.5525	50.4229	53.4891	56.7645	60.2638	64.0025
22	30.5368	32.3289	34.2480	36.3034	38.5052	40.8643	43.3923	46.1016	49.0057	52.1190	55.4568	59.0356	62.8733	66.9889	71.4027
23	32.4529	34.4604	36.6179	38.9370	41.4305	44.1118	46.9958	50.0982	53.4361	57.0279	60.8933	65.0537	69.5319	74.3529	79.5430
24	34.4265	36.6665	39.0826	41.6892	44.5020	47.5380	50.8156	54.3546	58.1767	62.3050	66.7648	71.5832	76.7898	82.4164	88.4973
25	36.4593	38.9499	41.6459	44.5652	47.7271	51.1526	54.8645	58.8877	63.2490	67.9779	73.1059	78.6678	84.7009	91.2459	98.3471
26	38.5530	41.3131	44.3117	47.5706	51.1135	54.9660	59.1564	63.7154	68.6765	74.0762	79.9544	86.3546	93.3240	100.9143	109.1818
27	40.7096	43.7591	47.0842	50.7113	54.4691	58.9891	63.7058	68.8569	74.4838	80.6319	87.3508	94.6947	102.7231	111.5012	121.0999
28	42.9309	46.2906	49.9676	53.9933	58.4026	63.2335	68.5281	74.4326	80.6977	87.6793	95.3388	103.7437	112.9682	123.0938	134.2099
29	45.2189	48.9108	52.9663	57.4230	62.3227	67.7114	73.6398	80.1642	87.3465	95.2553	103.9659	113.5620	124.1354	135.7877	148.6309
30	47.5754	51.6227	56.0849	61.0071	66.4388	72.4355	79.0582	86.3749	94.4608	103.3994	113.2832	124.2147	136.3075	149.6875	164.4940

Sinking Fund Factor

Number of Periods	3.0%	3.5%	4.0%	4.5%	5.0%	5.5%	6.0%	6.5%	7.0%	7.5%	8.0%	8.5%	9.0%	9.5%	10.0%
1	1.0000	1.0000	1.0000	1.0000	1.0000	1.0000	1.0000	1.0000	1.0000	1.0000	1.0000	1.0000	1.0000	1.0000	1.0000
2	0.4926	0.4914	0.4902	0.4890	0.4878	0.4866	0.4854	0.4843	0.4831	0.4819	0.4808	0.4796	0.4785	0.4773	0.4762
3	0.3235	0.3219	0.3203	0.3188	0.3172	0.3157	0.3141	0.3126	0.3111	0.3095	0.3080	0.3065	0.3051	0.3036	0.3021
4	0.2390	0.2373	0.2355	0.2337	0.2320	0.2303	0.2286	0.2269	0.2252	0.2236	0.2219	0.2203	0.2187	0.2171	0.2155
5	0.1884	0.1865	0.1846	0.1828	0.1810	0.1792	0.1774	0.1756	0.1739	0.1722	0.1705	0.1688	0.1671	0.1654	0.1638
6	0.1546	0.1527	0.1508	0.1489	0.1470	0.1452	0.1434	0.1416	0.1398	0.1380	0.1363	0.1346	0.1329	0.1313	0.1296
7	0.1305	0.1285	0.1266	0.1247	0.1228	0.1210	0.1191	0.1173	0.1156	0.1138	0.1121	0.1104	0.1087	0.1070	0.1054
8	0.1125	0.1105	0.1085	0.1066	0.1047	0.1029	0.1010	0.0992	0.0975	0.0957	0.0940	0.0923	0.0907	0.0890	0.0874
9	0.0984	0.0964	0.0945	0.0926	0.0907	0.0888	0.0870	0.0852	0.0835	0.0818	0.0801	0.0784	0.0768	0.0752	0.0736
10	0.0872	0.0852	0.0833	0.0814	0.0795	0.0777	0.0759	0.0741	0.0724	0.0707	0.0690	0.0674	0.0658	0.0643	0.0627
11	0.0781	0.0761	0.0741	0.0722	0.0704	0.0686	0.0668	0.0651	0.0634	0.0617	0.0601	0.0585	0.0569	0.0554	0.0540
12	0.0705	0.0685	0.0666	0.0647	0.0628	0.0610	0.0593	0.0576	0.0559	0.0543	0.0527	0.0512	0.0497	0.0482	0.0468
13	0.0640	0.0621	0.0601	0.0583	0.0565	0.0547	0.0530	0.0513	0.0497	0.0481	0.0465	0.0450	0.0436	0.0422	0.0408
14	0.0585	0.0566	0.0547	0.0528	0.0510	0.0493	0.0476	0.0459	0.0443	0.0428	0.0413	0.0398	0.0384	0.0371	0.0357
15	0.0538	0.0518	0.0499	0.0481	0.0463	0.0446	0.0430	0.0414	0.0398	0.0383	0.0368	0.0354	0.0341	0.0327	0.0315
16	0.0496	0.0477	0.0458	0.0440	0.0423	0.0406	0.0390	0.0374	0.0359	0.0344	0.0330	0.0316	0.0303	0.0290	0.0278
17	0.0460	0.0440	0.0422	0.0404	0.0387	0.0370	0.0354	0.0339	0.0324	0.0310	0.0296	0.0283	0.0270	0.0258	0.0247
18	0.0427	0.0408	0.0390	0.0372	0.0355	0.0339	0.0324	0.0309	0.0294	0.0280	0.0267	0.0254	0.0242	0.0230	0.0219
19	0.0398	0.0379	0.0361	0.0344	0.0327	0.0312	0.0296	0.0282	0.0268	0.0254	0.0241	0.0229	0.0217	0.0206	0.0195
20	0.0372	0.0354	0.0336	0.0319	0.0302	0.0287	0.0272	0.0258	0.0244	0.0231	0.0219	0.0207	0.0195	0.0185	0.0175
21	0.0349	0.0330	0.0313	0.0296	0.0280	0.0265	0.0250	0.0236	0.0223	0.0210	0.0198	0.0187	0.0176	0.0166	0.0156
22	0.0327	0.0309	0.0292	0.0275	0.0260	0.0245	0.0230	0.0217	0.0204	0.0192	0.0180	0.0169	0.0159	0.0149	0.0140
23	0.0308	0.0290	0.0273	0.0257	0.0241	0.0227	0.0213	0.0200	0.0187	0.0175	0.0164	0.0154	0.0144	0.0134	0.0126
24	0.0290	0.0273	0.0256	0.0240	0.0225	0.0210	0.0197	0.0184	0.0172	0.0161	0.0150	0.0140	0.0130	0.0121	0.0113
25	0.0274	0.0257	0.0240	0.0224	0.0210	0.0195	0.0182	0.0170	0.0158	0.0147	0.0137	0.0127	0.0118	0.0110	0.0102
26	0.0259	0.0242	0.0226	0.0210	0.0196	0.0182	0.0169	0.0157	0.0146	0.0135	0.0125	0.0116	0.0107	0.0099	0.0092
27	0.0246	0.0229	0.0212	0.0197	0.0183	0.0170	0.0157	0.0145	0.0134	0.0124	0.0114	0.0106	0.0097	0.0090	0.0083
28	0.0233	0.0216	0.0200	0.0185	0.0171	0.0158	0.0146	0.0135	0.0124	0.0114	0.0105	0.0096	0.0089	0.0081	0.0075
29	0.0221	0.0204	0.0189	0.0174	0.0160	0.0148	0.0136	0.0125	0.0114	0.0105	0.0096	0.0088	0.0081	0.0074	0.0067
30	0.0210	0.0194	0.0178	0.0164	0.0151	0.0138	0.0126	0.0116	0.0106	0.0097	0.0088	0.0081	0.0073	0.0067	0.0061

8 Mathematical Tables

Annual Equivalent Factor

Number of Periods	3.0%	3.5%	4.0%	4.5%	5.0%	5.5%	6.0%	6.5%	7.0%	7.5%	8.0%	8.5%	9.0%	9.5%	10.0%
1	1.0300	1.0350	1.0400	1.0450	1.0500	1.0550	1.0600	1.0650	1.0700	1.0750	1.0800	1.0850	1.0900	1.0950	1.1000
2	0.5226	0.5264	0.5302	0.5340	0.5378	0.5416	0.5454	0.5493	0.5531	0.5569	0.5608	0.5646	0.5685	0.5723	0.5762
3	0.3535	0.3569	0.3603	0.3638	0.3672	0.3707	0.3741	0.3776	0.3811	0.3845	0.3880	0.3915	0.3951	0.3986	0.4021
4	0.2690	0.2723	0.2755	0.2787	0.2820	0.2853	0.2886	0.2919	0.2952	0.2986	0.3019	0.3053	0.3087	0.3121	0.3155
5	0.2184	0.2215	0.2246	0.2278	0.2310	0.2342	0.2374	0.2406	0.2439	0.2472	0.2505	0.2538	0.2571	0.2604	0.2638
6	0.1846	0.1877	0.1908	0.1939	0.1970	0.2002	0.2034	0.2066	0.2098	0.2130	0.2163	0.2196	0.2229	0.2263	0.2296
7	0.1605	0.1635	0.1666	0.1697	0.1728	0.1760	0.1791	0.1823	0.1856	0.1888	0.1921	0.1954	0.1987	0.2020	0.2054
8	0.1425	0.1455	0.1485	0.1516	0.1547	0.1579	0.1610	0.1642	0.1675	0.1707	0.1740	0.1773	0.1807	0.1840	0.1874
9	0.1284	0.1314	0.1345	0.1376	0.1407	0.1438	0.1470	0.1502	0.1535	0.1568	0.1601	0.1634	0.1668	0.1702	0.1736
10	0.1172	0.1202	0.1233	0.1264	0.1295	0.1327	0.1359	0.1391	0.1424	0.1457	0.1490	0.1524	0.1558	0.1593	0.1627
11	0.1081	0.1111	0.1141	0.1172	0.1204	0.1236	0.1268	0.1301	0.1334	0.1367	0.1401	0.1435	0.1469	0.1504	0.1540
12	0.1005	0.1035	0.1066	0.1097	0.1128	0.1160	0.1193	0.1226	0.1259	0.1293	0.1327	0.1362	0.1397	0.1432	0.1468
13	0.0940	0.0971	0.1001	0.1033	0.1065	0.1097	0.1130	0.1163	0.1197	0.1231	0.1265	0.1300	0.1336	0.1372	0.1408
14	0.0885	0.0916	0.0947	0.0978	0.1010	0.1043	0.1076	0.1109	0.1143	0.1178	0.1213	0.1248	0.1284	0.1321	0.1357
15	0.0838	0.0868	0.0899	0.0931	0.0963	0.0996	0.1030	0.1064	0.1098	0.1133	0.1168	0.1204	0.1241	0.1277	0.1315
16	0.0796	0.0827	0.0858	0.0890	0.0923	0.0956	0.0990	0.1024	0.1059	0.1094	0.1130	0.1166	0.1203	0.1240	0.1278
17	0.0760	0.0790	0.0822	0.0854	0.0887	0.0920	0.0954	0.0989	0.1024	0.1060	0.1096	0.1133	0.1170	0.1208	0.1247
18	0.0727	0.0758	0.0790	0.0822	0.0855	0.0889	0.0924	0.0959	0.0994	0.1030	0.1067	0.1104	0.1142	0.1180	0.1219
19	0.0698	0.0729	0.0761	0.0794	0.0827	0.0862	0.0896	0.0932	0.0968	0.1004	0.1041	0.1079	0.1117	0.1156	0.1195
20	0.0672	0.0704	0.0736	0.0769	0.0802	0.0837	0.0872	0.0908	0.0944	0.0981	0.1019	0.1057	0.1095	0.1135	0.1175
21	0.0649	0.0680	0.0713	0.0746	0.0780	0.0815	0.0850	0.0886	0.0923	0.0960	0.0998	0.1037	0.1076	0.1116	0.1156
22	0.0627	0.0659	0.0692	0.0725	0.0760	0.0795	0.0830	0.0867	0.0904	0.0942	0.0980	0.1019	0.1059	0.1099	0.1140
23	0.0608	0.0640	0.0673	0.0707	0.0741	0.0777	0.0813	0.0850	0.0887	0.0925	0.0964	0.1004	0.1044	0.1084	0.1126
24	0.0590	0.0623	0.0656	0.0690	0.0725	0.0760	0.0797	0.0834	0.0872	0.0911	0.0950	0.0990	0.1030	0.1071	0.1113
25	0.0574	0.0607	0.0640	0.0674	0.0710	0.0745	0.0782	0.0820	0.0858	0.0897	0.0937	0.0977	0.1018	0.1060	0.1102
26	0.0559	0.0592	0.0626	0.0660	0.0696	0.0732	0.0769	0.0807	0.0846	0.0885	0.0925	0.0966	0.1007	0.1049	0.1092
27	0.0546	0.0579	0.0612	0.0647	0.0683	0.0720	0.0757	0.0795	0.0834	0.0874	0.0914	0.0956	0.0997	0.1040	0.1083
28	0.0533	0.0566	0.0600	0.0635	0.0671	0.0708	0.0746	0.0785	0.0824	0.0864	0.0905	0.0946	0.0989	0.1031	0.1075
29	0.0521	0.0554	0.0589	0.0624	0.0660	0.0698	0.0736	0.0775	0.0814	0.0855	0.0896	0.0938	0.0981	0.1024	0.1067
30	0.0510	0.0544	0.0578	0.0614	0.0651	0.0688	0.0726	0.0766	0.0806	0.0847	0.0888	0.0931	0.0973	0.1017	0.1061

Present Value Factor

Number of Periods	3.0%	3.5%	4.0%	4.5%	5.0%	5.5%	6.0%	6.5%	7.0%	7.5%	8.0%	8.5%	9.0%	9.5%	10.0%
1	0.9709	0.9662	0.9615	0.9569	0.9524	0.9479	0.9434	0.9390	0.9346	0.9302	0.9259	0.9217	0.9174	0.9132	0.9091
2	0.9426	0.9335	0.9246	0.9157	0.9070	0.8985	0.8900	0.8817	0.8734	0.8653	0.8573	0.8495	0.8417	0.8340	0.8264
3	0.9151	0.9019	0.8890	0.8763	0.8638	0.8516	0.8396	0.8278	0.8163	0.8050	0.7938	0.7829	0.7722	0.7617	0.7513
4	0.8885	0.8714	0.8548	0.8386	0.8227	0.8072	0.7921	0.7773	0.7629	0.7488	0.7350	0.7216	0.7084	0.6956	0.6830
5	0.8626	0.8420	0.8219	0.8025	0.7835	0.7651	0.7473	0.7299	0.7130	0.6966	0.6806	0.6650	0.6499	0.6352	0.6209
6	0.8375	0.8135	0.7903	0.7679	0.7462	0.7252	0.7050	0.6853	0.6663	0.6480	0.6302	0.6129	0.5963	0.5801	0.5645
7	0.8131	0.7860	0.7599	0.7348	0.7107	0.6874	0.6651	0.6435	0.6227	0.6028	0.5835	0.5649	0.5470	0.5298	0.5132
8	0.7894	0.7594	0.7307	0.7032	0.6768	0.6516	0.6274	0.6042	0.5820	0.5607	0.5403	0.5207	0.5019	0.4838	0.4665
9	0.7664	0.7337	0.7026	0.6729	0.6446	0.6176	0.5919	0.5674	0.5439	0.5216	0.5002	0.4799	0.4604	0.4418	0.4241
10	0.7441	0.7089	0.6756	0.6439	0.6139	0.5854	0.5584	0.5327	0.5083	0.4852	0.4632	0.4423	0.4224	0.4035	0.3855
11	0.7224	0.6849	0.6496	0.6162	0.5847	0.5549	0.5268	0.5002	0.4751	0.4513	0.4289	0.4076	0.3875	0.3685	0.3505
12	0.7014	0.6618	0.6246	0.5897	0.5568	0.5260	0.4970	0.4697	0.4440	0.4199	0.3971	0.3757	0.3555	0.3365	0.3186
13	0.6810	0.6394	0.6006	0.5643	0.5303	0.4986	0.4688	0.4410	0.4150	0.3906	0.3677	0.3463	0.3262	0.3073	0.2897
14	0.6611	0.6178	0.5775	0.5400	0.5051	0.4726	0.4423	0.4141	0.3878	0.3633	0.3405	0.3191	0.2992	0.2807	0.2633
15	0.6419	0.5969	0.5553	0.5167	0.4810	0.4479	0.4173	0.3888	0.3624	0.3380	0.3152	0.2941	0.2745	0.2563	0.2394
16	0.6232	0.5767	0.5339	0.4945	0.4581	0.4246	0.3936	0.3651	0.3387	0.3144	0.2919	0.2711	0.2519	0.2341	0.2176
17	0.6050	0.5572	0.5134	0.4732	0.4363	0.4024	0.3714	0.3428	0.3166	0.2925	0.2703	0.2499	0.2311	0.2138	0.1978
18	0.5874	0.5384	0.4936	0.4528	0.4155	0.3815	0.3503	0.3219	0.2959	0.2720	0.2502	0.2303	0.2120	0.1952	0.1799
19	0.5703	0.5202	0.4746	0.4333	0.3957	0.3616	0.3305	0.3022	0.2765	0.2531	0.2317	0.2122	0.1945	0.1783	0.1635
20	0.5537	0.5026	0.4564	0.4146	0.3769	0.3427	0.3118	0.2838	0.2584	0.2354	0.2145	0.1956	0.1784	0.1628	0.1486
21	0.5375	0.4856	0.4388	0.3968	0.3589	0.3249	0.2942	0.2665	0.2415	0.2190	0.1987	0.1803	0.1637	0.1487	0.1351
22	0.5219	0.4692	0.4220	0.3797	0.3418	0.3079	0.2775	0.2502	0.2257	0.2037	0.1839	0.1662	0.1502	0.1358	0.1228
23	0.5067	0.4533	0.4057	0.3634	0.3256	0.2919	0.2618	0.2349	0.2109	0.1895	0.1703	0.1531	0.1378	0.1240	0.1117
24	0.4919	0.4380	0.3901	0.3477	0.3101	0.2767	0.2470	0.2206	0.1971	0.1763	0.1577	0.1412	0.1264	0.1133	0.1015
25	0.4776	0.4231	0.3751	0.3327	0.2953	0.2622	0.2330	0.2071	0.1842	0.1640	0.1460	0.1301	0.1160	0.1034	0.0923
26	0.4637	0.4088	0.3607	0.3184	0.2812	0.2486	0.2198	0.1945	0.1722	0.1525	0.1352	0.1199	0.1064	0.0945	0.0839
27	0.4502	0.3950	0.3468	0.3047	0.2678	0.2356	0.2074	0.1826	0.1609	0.1419	0.1252	0.1105	0.0976	0.0863	0.0763
28	0.4371	0.3817	0.3335	0.2916	0.2551	0.2233	0.1956	0.1715	0.1504	0.1320	0.1159	0.1019	0.0895	0.0788	0.0693
29	0.4243	0.3687	0.3207	0.2790	0.2429	0.2117	0.1846	0.1610	0.1406	0.1228	0.1073	0.0939	0.0822	0.0719	0.0630
30	0.4120	0.3563	0.3083	0.2670	0.2314	0.2006	0.1741	0.1512	0.1314	0.1142	0.0994	0.0865	0.0754	0.0657	0.0573

Annuity Present Value Factor

Number of Periods	3.0%	3.5%	4.0%	4.5%	5.0%	5.5%	6.0%	6.5%	7.0%	7.5%	8.0%	8.5%	9.0%	9.5%	10.0%
1	0.9709	0.9662	0.9615	0.9569	0.9524	0.9479	0.9434	0.9390	0.9346	0.9302	0.9259	0.9217	0.9174	0.9132	0.9091
2	1.9135	1.8997	1.8861	1.8727	1.8594	1.8463	1.8334	1.8206	1.8080	1.7956	1.7833	1.7711	1.7591	1.7473	1.7355
3	2.8286	2.8016	2.7751	2.7490	2.7232	2.6979	2.6730	2.6485	2.6243	2.6005	2.5771	2.5540	2.5313	2.5089	2.4869
4	3.7171	3.6731	3.6299	3.5875	3.5460	3.5052	3.4651	3.4258	3.3872	3.3493	3.3121	3.2756	3.2397	3.2045	3.1699
5	4.5797	4.5151	4.4518	4.3900	4.3295	4.2703	4.2124	4.1557	4.1002	4.0459	3.9927	3.9406	3.8897	3.8397	3.7908
6	5.4172	5.3286	5.2421	5.1579	5.0757	4.9955	4.9173	4.8410	4.7665	4.6938	4.6229	4.5536	4.4859	4.4198	4.3553
7	6.2303	6.1145	6.0021	5.8927	5.7864	5.6830	5.5824	5.4845	5.3893	5.2966	5.2064	5.1185	5.0330	4.9496	4.8684
8	7.0197	6.8740	6.7327	6.5959	6.4632	6.3346	6.2098	6.0888	5.9713	5.8573	5.7466	5.6392	5.5348	5.4334	5.3349
9	7.7861	7.6077	7.4353	7.2688	7.1078	6.9522	6.8017	6.6561	6.5152	6.3789	6.2469	6.1191	5.9952	5.8753	5.7590
10	8.5302	8.3166	8.1109	7.9127	7.7217	7.5376	7.3601	7.1888	7.0236	6.8641	6.7101	6.5613	6.4177	6.2788	6.1446
11	9.2526	9.0016	8.7605	8.5289	8.3064	8.0925	7.8869	7.6890	7.4987	7.3154	7.1390	6.9690	6.8052	6.6473	6.4951
12	9.9540	9.6633	9.3851	9.1186	8.8633	8.6185	8.3838	8.1587	7.9427	7.7353	7.5361	7.3447	7.1607	6.9838	6.8137
13	10.6350	10.3027	9.9856	9.6829	9.3936	9.1171	8.8527	8.5997	8.3577	8.1258	7.9038	7.6910	7.4869	7.2912	7.1034
14	11.2961	10.9205	10.5631	10.2228	9.8986	9.5896	9.2950	9.0138	8.7455	8.4892	8.2442	8.0101	7.7862	7.5719	7.3667
15	11.9379	11.5174	11.1184	10.7395	10.3797	10.0376	9.7122	9.4027	9.1079	8.8271	8.5595	8.3042	8.0607	7.8282	7.6061
16	12.5611	12.0941	11.6523	11.2340	10.8378	10.4622	10.1059	9.7678	9.4466	9.1415	8.8514	8.5753	8.3126	8.0623	7.8237
17	13.1661	12.6513	12.1657	11.7072	11.2741	10.8646	10.4773	10.1106	9.7632	9.4340	9.1216	8.8252	8.5436	8.2760	8.0216
18	13.7535	13.1897	12.6593	12.1600	11.6896	11.2461	10.8276	10.4325	10.0591	9.7060	9.3719	9.0555	8.7556	8.4713	8.2014
19	14.3238	13.7098	13.1339	12.5933	12.0853	11.6077	11.1581	10.7347	10.3356	9.9591	9.6036	9.2677	8.9501	8.6496	8.3649
20	14.8775	14.2124	13.5903	13.0079	12.4622	11.9504	11.4699	11.0185	10.5940	10.1945	9.8181	9.4633	9.1285	8.8124	8.5136
21	15.4150	14.6980	14.0292	13.4047	12.8212	12.2752	11.7641	11.2850	10.8355	10.4135	10.0168	9.6436	9.2922	8.9611	8.6487
22	15.9369	15.1671	14.4511	13.7844	13.1630	12.5832	12.0416	11.5352	11.0612	10.6172	10.2007	9.8098	9.4424	9.0969	8.7715
23	16.4436	15.6204	14.8568	14.1478	13.4886	12.8750	12.3034	11.7701	11.2722	10.8067	10.3711	9.9629	9.5802	9.2209	8.8832
24	16.9355	16.0584	15.2470	14.4955	13.7986	13.1517	12.5504	11.9907	11.4693	10.9830	10.5288	10.1041	9.7066	9.3341	8.9847
25	17.4131	16.4815	15.6221	14.8282	14.0939	13.4139	12.7834	12.1979	11.6536	11.1469	10.6748	10.2342	9.8226	9.4376	9.0770
26	17.8768	16.8904	15.9828	15.1466	14.3752	13.6625	13.0032	12.3924	11.8258	11.2995	10.8100	10.3541	9.9290	9.5320	9.1609
27	18.3270	17.2854	16.3296	15.4513	14.6430	13.8981	13.2105	12.5750	11.9867	11.4414	10.9352	10.4646	10.0266	9.6183	9.2372
28	18.7641	17.6670	16.6631	15.7429	14.8981	14.1214	13.4062	12.7465	12.1371	11.5734	11.0511	10.5665	10.1161	9.6971	9.3066
29	19.1885	18.0358	16.9837	16.0219	15.1411	14.3331	13.5907	12.9075	12.2777	11.6962	11.1584	10.6603	10.1983	9.7690	9.3696
30	19.6004	18.3920	17.2920	16.2889	15.3725	14.5337	13.7648	13.0587	12.4090	11.8104	11.2578	10.7468	10.2737	9.8347	9.4269

9 Index

A

accounting rate of return	29
accounting rate of return method	29
annual equivalent factor	60, 62
annuity	76
annuity future value factor	59, 62
annuity method	76
annuity present value factor	59, 62

C

capital costs	13
cash flow	34
classification of investments	3
comparison of alternatives	12
comparison of cost per unit	12
comparison of costs per period	12
complete financial plan	66, 157
correction method	111
cost comparison method	11
cost functions	18
critical discount rate	79
critical values	18, 114, 116

D

decision tree analysis	123
depreciation	13
differential investments	69
discounting methods	3, 55
discounting payback method	87

F

financing	2, 65
fixed planning	124
flexible planning	124, 129
future value factor	61
future value interest factor	57

I

imputed interest	14
inflation	154
internal rate of return	
arithmetic approximation	81
calculation using Excel	82
graphical approximation	80
internal rate of return method	79

L

linear interpolation	80

M

macroeconomic net present value method	163
mathematical tables	58
Monte Carlo simulation	118

N

net present value	64
net present value method	62
nominal interest rate	155
non-discounting methods	3, 11

P

paradox of taxation 152
payback method 33
payback period 33
present value factor 59, 61
profit 25
profit comparison method 24
profitability index 65
public investments 163

R

random numbers 120
real interest rate 155
reference point 56
reinvestment assumption 65, 86
relevant costs with regard to the replacement decision 20
replacement decision 12

S

risk 110
risk analysis 118
risk profile 122
running costs 13

S

salvage values 16
scenario analysis 114
scoring model 160
sensitivity analysis 114
simulation model 120
sinking fund factor 60, 62

T

taxation 150

U

uncertainty 110